Proven Health Tips Encyclopedia

IMPORTANT NOTICE

This manual is intended as a reference volume only, not as a medical guide or a reference for self treatment. You should always seek competent medical advice from a doctor if you suspect a problem.
This book is intended as an educational device to keep you informed of the latest medical knowledge. It is not intended to serve as a substitute for changing the treatment or advice of your doctor. You should never make medical changes without first consulting your doctor.

Printed in the United States of America 0 9 8 7 6 5 4 3 2 1

TABLE OF CONTENTS

    Fatty Foods
    Don't drink with your meal
    The Fiber Fix
    Switch from white to wheat
    Stop eating, and eat less
    Don't smoke after a meal
    Watch yourself

    First, let's get rid of the myths
    So what can you do about acne?
    Get Pregnant
    Hit the beach
    Ice Pack It!
    Stay Clean
    To squeeze, or not to squeeze
    Over-the counter acne products
    Avoid these foods
    Foods to heal acne?
    Good sources of zinc are:
    Treat your skin as you would any other body organ

    The Big Three Life Extenders
    The Power of Friendship
    Shed That Weight!
    Studies Prove That Meditation Keeps You Young
    Special Discussion on Aging: Mind Over Matter
    Consider this:

Introduction to Health Tips Encyclopedia

So tell me, how do you feel?

Terrible, you say? In that case, I want to have a talk with you. Come on, pull up a chair and listen for a minute.

If you feel terrible, if you seem to be sick all the time, if you're depressed, if you drag yourself painfully from one end of the day to the other, if you get more than your share of colds or flu or PMS or allergies, why not do something about it — today?

That's what I did. I used to feel awful all the time. You name it, I had it — from the corns on the bottom of my feet to the headaches and dandruff at the top of my head ...

... not to mention my swollen joints, low energy level, and a stomach that would turn sour over the simplest of meals, or sometimes even a glass of milk.

But no more. Today, I feel great. No, that's not quite true. I feel fantastic! I have lots of energy, I have a body with no aches or complaints, and a stomach that can rejoice over a spicy Cajun dinner or a couple of well-seasoned tacos.

How did I do it? How did I go from a certified physical disaster area to a picture of glowing good health? Well, it's difficult to name any one or two things, but if I had to pick something as the key it would be that I started to pay attention.

More specifically, I started paying attention to what my

body was constantly trying to tell me. I realized that every time my body had an ache or pain, it was saying: "Hey! What are your doing to me? I need help! Please listen to me!"

For example, when my heart started to flutter, I begin to notice that my palpitations usually appeared later in the afternoon, and often when I was gulping down my 15th cup of coffee for the day.

"Wait a minute," I thought, looking at the cup in my hand and listening to my heart. "Maybe my body has had enough of this stuff for the day. One or two cups is great to get me going, but do I have to drink it all day?"

So when I cut down on coffee, my heart stopped fluttering. And lo and behold, when I cut down on coffee, I also noticed that my joints didn't swell up as much, and my stomach seemed to be a lot less irritated.

Once my stomach stopped being irritated, I found it easier to eat decent meals. When I did that, my energy level went up. When my energy level went up, I found that I slept better at nights. When I started getting better sleep and nutrition, I found I had fewer headaches and ...

... are you starting to get the picture?

In a nutshell, I found that a lot of my sicknesses actually had a lot of simple causes, and that there were many simple, easy and cost-free things I could do to improve my health.

I didn't have to pay a doctor a big chunk of money or take all kinds of prescription drugs — which often have side effects worse than their cures — to find my way back to a fit and healthy life.

I started writing things down. Whenever I encountered an ache or pain, I took out a clean sheet of paper, wrote the particular problem at the top of the page and then went looking for ways to deal with it. My search took me to the library, to people who knew about folk medicine, to friends I have in the medical profession, and to my own trial and error experiments. Sometimes my research was exhaustive, other times I found that answers were right in front of my nose.

The result was an ever-growing scrapbook of medical conditions and the simple, every day treatments I found that could make them better. Over the years, I started to get a pretty thick stack of pages, and at the urging of a friend, I decided to compile them all in the form of a book. The result is the book you are holding in your hands.

The Health Care Tips Encyclopedia is a compilation of dozens of common, every day medical problems — from abdominal pains to yeast infections — and a host of possible solutions or suggestions you can use to deal with them.

Of course, no book, no matter who it's written by, is a total substitute for professional health care. In these pages, I don't offer a cure for cancer — just many ways you can prevent cancer from happening to you. I don't have a cure for diabetes, but I do tell you about the kind of diet that can make living with this incurable disease a lot easier. I don't give directions on where you can find the "Fountain of Youth", but I do offer several ways you can add many healthy years to your life, and ways to make you feel younger than you are right now.

And much more.

Please note: I have been as careful and diligent as possible in providing accurate reproduction of health information, but this book does not constitute medical advice and should not be construed as such. We cannot guarantee the safety or effectiveness of any drug or treatment or advice mentioned. The only intent of this book is to provide you with helpful information that may point you in a new direction in your search for better health.

The world of professional medicine is advancing so rapidly that what is considered true today may be overturned tomorrow. We strongly recommend that you contact your personal physician before taking or discontinuing any medications, or before treating yourself in any way.

Perhaps more than anything, reading these pages will give you a better understanding about what is ailing you, and perhaps have a new attitude towards dealing with your medical problem.

Remember, your body belongs to you and no one else, you are responsible for it, and only you can truly listen to its internal language to find out what it's trying to tell you. Even before you tell a doctor what is wrong with you, you must have the ability to look into yourself and describe what you are feeling.

We hope this book helps you do that ... and we fervently wish you a long, healthy and prosperous life filled with joy and serenity.

Abdominal Pains

Abdominal, or stomach pains can be a real ...er ... pain, and they can often be scary because they cause so much discomfort and mental distress. Many people automatically assume the worst when they have abdominal pains — ulcers, appendicitis, or something worse.

Generally, abdominal pains come in three broad categories:

(1) An acute problem, that is, a pain that comes on suddenly which requires immediate, emergency action, such as appendicitis.

(2) A chronic condition, such as an ulcer, kidney infection, colon problem, or others.

(3) A simple nervous or upset stomach brought on by indigestion, stress or a poor diet.

Fortunately, the best chance is that your stomach ache is of the third category. Obviously, sudden, extreme will prompt you to seek emergency medical care.

Most often, however, your stomach pains are due to ordinary causes, such as overeating, food your stomach doesn't like, physical or mental stress which increases the acid level in your stomach, and so on. The key is to monitor your condition. If your pain is long lasting, persists for several days or more, then you may have a serious medical problem, such as an ulcer, colon problem, gall bladder problem, irritable bowel syndrome, and so on. It's likely that you can fix your abdominal pains quickly by trying a few easy things first:

Fatty foods

Beware of greasy, fatty foods. These are perhaps the most frequent cause of abdominal pains. If you are eating a high fat or greasy meal — stop. The sooner you stop, the sooner your stomach pain will go away. If it doesn't an ordinary off-the-shelf antacid will most likely help.

Don't drink with your meal

Drinking water or any other drink with your meal is poor for digestion because it dilutes the natural digestive fluids in your stomach and interferes with the processing of food in your body. Stay away from liquids an hour before and after meals. Your stomach will fare much better as a result.

The Fiber Fix

In general, though, limit your intake of fatty foods. Diets high in fiber are an excellent way to prevent stomach problems, or repair stomachs that are already damaged. Wheat bran, beans, bulgar and rice promote passage of food through the digestive tract. Including them in your daily diet may fix abdominal pains for good.

Switch from white to wheat

White bread is much more difficult for your stomach to digest. Switching from white to whole wheat bread will make a big difference to your stomach.

Stop eating, and eat less

Simple, common sense advice, but — hey! — it works. Your mother used to tell you not to gulp your food or to stuff yourself with junk food or any kind of food. Simply stop eating now and there's a good chance your stomach pains will soon stop.

Don't smoke after a meal

One of the worst things you can do for your stomach is to light up a cigarette after a meal. The nicotine and other chemicals of tobacco smoke actually put the breaks on the digestive process, but allows your stomach to go on producing acids to dissolve food. The result — a hummer of a stomach ache. Forget the cigarette and you may be able to forget abdominal pain and heartburn.

Watch yourself

Of course, use common sense when dealing with abdominal pains, and be sure that's just where your pain is! It's not uncommon, for example, for a severe migraine headache to produce vomiting and upset stomach. But in that case, there's nothing wrong with your stomach, but with your head! Also, your pain may be more in your side or ribs than your stomach. See if you can't point directly to where it hurts.

If your problems are foods or mental stress, then your pain should go away once these problems have been removed. If your pain persists, then maybe it's time to see a doctor.

ACNE

This skin disease is, without a doubt, the No. 1 psychological nightmare for millions of teen-agers. The term acne encompasses what are usually called pimples, whiteheads and blackheads.

For the most part, acne is a problem for adolescents because of the hormones associated with reaching puberty. In fact, three out of four American teen-agers have at least a mild case of acne, although many adults suffer from this skin disease. Some adults develop their first case of acne in their twenties or thirties.

Acne is closely linked to the male hormone testosterone, which boys produce rapidly when they approach puberty. So why do females get acne? Because they have testosterone in their bodies, too! Although females have smaller amounts of testosterone, some have enough to make acne a real problem for them as adolescents. But Mother Nature does not play favorites when it comes to acne. The female hormone, estrogen, has also been linked to these unpleasant skin blemishes, especially in adult women approaching menstruation. Women are more prone to what is called "adult acne" than males, perhaps because of their estrogen levels.

While acne rarely develops into a life threatening medical problem, the psychological factor of the disease, especially for image conscious teen-agers, is enormous. That makes a treatment for acne — and a caring and understanding attitude for your teen-ager's plight — extremely important. Fortunately, there is a lot you can do to fight this daunting nuisance of the skin.

First, let's get rid of the myths

Good news! Chocolate and sex do not cause, or increase the severity of acne! How could any teen-ager get by without ... chocolate? And, contrary to popular belief, dirty, oily hair and skin does not cause acne, nor does eating greasy foods, including the deep-fried stuff. Acne is largely the result of genetics. You inherit your susceptibility to this disease from your parents, which also makes it particularly hard to get rid of.

So what can you do about acne?

The most important thing to remember that skin is your body's largest organ. Most of us are used to thinking in terms of hearts and kidneys, lungs and livers — but the skin also comprises of a whole organ within itself, even though it doesn't come in a compact shape like other organs.

Just as we treat our heart or lungs with the proper exercise and diet, so too the skin should be given the food, oxygen and exercise it needs to maintain its optimum level of health.

We'll give you a few more tips on skin diet shortly, but first, let's look at some specific things you can do right away to treat problems with acne.

Get Pregnant

That's right — get pregnant. No, this is not a joke (although probably not a good solution either. Are you teen-agers listening?) But the truth is, pregnant women often find that as their body chemistry changes during pregnancy, their skin problems clear up as well.

Speaking of pregnancy, the experts disagree on whether or not oral contraceptives help or hurt the occurrence of acne. In researching this book, we found many direct contradiction from one source to the next. Some studies show that certain contraceptives increase acne, while others suppress it. I guess you'll have to rely on your own experience in this case, since the experts are divided on the issue.

Hit the beach

Perhaps one of the best, no-cost treatments for acne is a

bit of sunshine. A moderate amount of sun almost always has a beneficial effect on skin clarity. Too much sun, however, will lead to a boomerang effect. As you know, too much sun dries out the skin, causes skin-cell damage and can actually make skin more susceptible to acne in the long run. So catch a few rays, but definitely don't overdo it!

Ice Pack It!

Here is a plan of attack, especially for those who are already all too familiar with the pain and suffering of acne. When you get "that feeling" on your skin that a pimple or some kind of outbreak is about the happen, get an ice pack on it before the skin disruption appears. Five to 10 minutes will do it. An ice-pack may prevent the blemish from developing in the first place, and will help maintain the integrity of your skin cell walls.

Stay Clean

I know, we already said that dirty, oily skin does not cause acne ... but that does not mean keeping a clean face can't prevent acne from becoming worse. In acne, the oil glands are overactive. Keeping them clean as often as possible will reduce acne. The problem is, however, that glands can secrete more oil within an hour after washing. Thus, keeping skin washed clean often is advisable — but please maintain a sense of moderation and common sense as you work your cleanliness program. Washing your face once an hour is probably not a good idea. Just as getting too much sun will eventually lead to more acne, a compulsive, overactive face scrubber might exceed the benefits of keeping the skin clean. Note: scrub your face gently, and use a soap that contains hexachlorophene, which is available over the counter.

To squeeze, or not to squeeze

The answer? Sometimes yes, and sometimes no. Do squeeze a pimple when it has a soft, central (usually yellowish) pus head on it. Prick the center (gently and not deeply! — just break the surface!) first with a pin sterilized by a flame, then use a tissue to squeeze out as much pus as you can. This will greatly speed up the rate of healing. Don't force it! If a pimple is red and hard and resists the point of your pin, leave it alone!

Over-the counter acne products

What can we tell you about these products that you don't already know? Probably not much. No doubt, you've experimented with them already and you know what the results are. A bit of advise that will come to you as no revelation: don't expect miracles!

Don't be over sold by the claims of advertisers and producers of these products. If there really was a quick, easy fix for acne that came in a neat little jar, believe us, it would be on the market right now and someone would be making a mint selling it. If you do choose to use over-the-counter products, however, choose ones that contain the following:

Hexachlorophene   benzalkonium chloride
phenol   salicylic acid
camphor   menthol
sulfur   aluminum oxide
benzoyl peroxide   zinc (an oral, vitamin
    supplement)

Avoid make-up

Ironically, the one thing most people with acne want to do is cover it up with thick layers of make-up — bad idea.

Make-up will make your acne worse. It will clog pores and deprive your skin of oxygen. The more make-up, the more irritated the skin. Sorry.

Avoid these foods

Surprisingly, it is not the sweets and greasy foods that have been blamed for so long that may make acne worse. It is foods that contain high amounts of iodine that may be the real culprit in acne flare-ups. Here are some of the biggest culprits:

Iodized salt	Beef liver
Tortilla Chips	Butter
Kelp	Most shellfish, including shrimp
Asparagus	Broccoli
White onions	Turkey (white meat)

And there are many more. To find the iodine levels in any food, consult a food nutrition guide, which are available in any library.

Foods to heal acne?

Much has been made about diet and how it affects acne, but this continues to be a very elusive area of study. The best available evidence and real-life experience suggests that foods high in vitamin A and zinc offer the greatest help with acne. These food are highest in Vitamin A:

Apricots	Green beans
Broccoli	Cantaloupe
Carrots	Peaches
Spinach	Sweet potatoes
Pumpkins	Squash

In general, you can assume if a fruit or vegetable is orange or yellow, it is most likely high in vitamin A.

Good sources of zinc are:

Lamb	Lean pork
Brown rice	Lean beef
Salmon	Baked potato

Treat your skin as you would any other body organ

Now let's return to the fact that your skin is an organ, as is your heart, lungs, kidney and others. Give your skin all the basic nutrients it needs to function properly, and avoid all the things that will impair it's function. In general, heavy red meats, tobacco, alcohol, make-up, dark skin tans will all cause harm to your skin. Try to eat more fruits and vegetables, especially those rich in vitamin A and beta-carotene. Get a lot of fresh air, a lot of exercise to oxygenate your skin — and most importantly — don't think of your skin as an enemy, even if your skin is covered with angry red pimples. Maybe it's trying to tell you something. Listen to your skin and send good thoughts to it — thoughts of healing and kindness. You will be surprised at the response.

Abrasions

You know what this is — it's when a child skins a knee. An abrasion is a common injury that all mothers are familiar with. When the skin is scraped away, but not sliced or lacerated, that's an abrasion. It is rarely dangerous as long as it is cleaned gently and covered with a bandage. Don't waste your money on antiseptic sprays or ointments, or by going to a doctor. But applying some hydrogen peroxide with a cotton ball will greatly speed up the healing process. Remember to keep the wound clean and covered until a scab forms and new skin grows beneath. Of course, a hug and a kiss and a kind "there, there" will do light years of good.

Acupressure

Here is something that we're really excited about. Anyone who is seeking zero-cost, effective medical help should know about the powerful, ancient oriental healing practice of acupressure. You probably have heard of acupuncture — sticking needles in the body at strategic points to relieve pain and to treat an endless variety of ailments.

Well, acupressure is a close cousin to acupuncture, but it has several advantages over its prickly relative.

(1) First, you don't have to have your body poked all over with needles. Need we say any more about that?

(2) Second, acupuncture requires the services of a highly skilled and highly expensive specialist. Acupressure, on the other hand, can be done by absolutely anyone; it can even be done by yourself if you have no one to help you.

(3) Acupressure relieves muscular tension, which greatly improves overall circulation through the body. Specifically, acupressure affects four systems of the body: heart function; respiration, blood composition and the digestive system. Stimulating and regulating these four vital functions promotes physical calmness and mental alertness — which sets the stage for healing and increased health.

(4) Scientists believe the acupressure on the surface of the body triggers the release of pain suppressing

chemicals in the brain, including enkephalins (meaning "in the head") and endorphines (meaning "the morphine within").

(5) A simple five-minute session of acupressure can:

  (a) Stop pain immediately
  (b) increase energy and mental alertness.
  (c) relieve a stiff neck and shoulders.
  (d) relieve mental tension.
  (e) cure headaches and relieve strained eyes.
  (f) get rid of depression

Here's a 10-minute, 10-step acupressure treatment that will make you feel great all over! Give it a try!

(1) First you want to apply acupressure to both shoulders. Use your right hand to firmly squeeze your left shoulder muscle on a point halfway between the base of the neck and the shoulder tip. Do it for 15-20 seconds, and squeeze just hard enough to cause a bit of pleasurable pain, but don't overdo it. Then switch to the right shoulder and do the same thing with your left hand, remembering to concentrate on the midpoint of the shoulder.

Benefits: The shoulder point has long been associated with recovering a lost voice due to cold, flu or throat infection. It also relieves fatigue and anxiety.

(2) Next the temples. Simply put your three middle fingers on each temple, close your eyes and press firmly for about 15 seconds. This will relax muscles elsewhere in your body, especially the neck.

Benefits: Can lessen pain anywhere in the body because it relieves tension in the neck and elsewhere.

(3) Next let's work on the skull. With both hands, press just

beneath the base of your skull on the back of your head with your thumbs. Press upward into the base of the outer part of the skull. To obtain the right pressure, tilt your head back. You will feel a dull pain when you are pressing the correct points.

Benefits: Relieves mental tension and headaches. Improves memory and alertness.

(4) The ears. There are several points on the ear that can be stimulated with acupressure to achieve a variety of results. The fist point is directly behind the ear. Fold your ear forward and place your finger on the mastoid bone, which is just behind your ear. You'll feel it. Working this point relieves a simple earache.

Another ear exercise involves using the thumbs and index fingers of both hands to massage the outer, fleshy part of your ears. Begin at the lower end of the ear lobes and move to the upper part of the ears. Do this twice, taking about 15 seconds each time. This exercise will energize and clear the mind.

A third ear point is on the "bridge" of the ear, about a third of the way down from the top and near the front of the ear. Exercising this point several times a day can greatly decrease your craving for tobacco.

(5) Now the eyes. Rapid relief for aching eyes can easily be achieved by pressing on a point just in the inside corner of your eye, next to your nose. The left point treats the right eye and vica versa.

Next, rub around the outer rims of both eyes, using medium pressure applied with the middle fingers. Begin at the inner corners of the eyes and move first along the lower part of the orbit toward the temples.

After the above two procedures, all your eyestrain or pain will disappear!

(6) Hand-web press. With thumb and index finger, firmly squeeze the fleshiest part of the webbing between the index finger and the thumb of the left hand. Do each hand for 5 - 15 seconds.

Benefits: Relieves headaches, sinus congestion and arthritis pain.

(7) Cheek press: With your middle and index fingers, press along the lower part of the cheek bone. Begin next to the nose and move outward to the ears. Take about 15 seconds and do it three times. Benefits: Relieves sinus congestion and tension in the face and head, and improves the complexion.

Benefits: Relieves sinus congestion, head and face tension and improves complexion.

(8) To relieve a headache, massage the point where you normally take your pulse, but move a little higher, toward the elbow. Working this point will relieve a headache in the forehead or temples. For a headache on the nape of the neck behind the head, put pressure on a point on the little finger side of the hand. Half bend your hand and massage the point just on the wrist side of the crease your little finger makes.

(9) To break yourself out of a depression, try putting pressure on a point on your torso that is halfway between the base of the ribs and the navel. Do it while lying on your back. Also, rubbing the folds of your wrists beneath your hands can lift your spirits from a black mood.

(10) To treat stomach pain, massage a point below and inside your knee, along the back edge of the tibia Find the

point where the edge of the bone suddenly bends inward.

Acupressure is a complex, highly developed ancient practice which reaches far back into the history of the ancient Chinese. In addition to the 10 points described above, there are many other points which have been shown to help everything from sexual disfunction to mental instability. Elsewhere in the book, we will point out other acupressure treatments where they are appropriate. But taking some time once a day or every other day to work the 10 points described here may be all you need to stay completely healthy in all aspects of your life.

Aging

Do you think it's possible for human beings to easily live 120 years? 130? or even older? The best scientific evidence seems to tell us: "Why not?"

Experts on aging tell us that there is no reason why the human body cannot last at least twice as long as it does. Today the average life span of men and women is somewhere in the seventies, with women living about 6-8 years longer than men. What most people don't realize is that just 100 or so years ago, the average life span was about half of what it is today.

If we have doubled our life spans once, why can't we do it again?

Maybe we can. Barring being killed in accidents or developing catastrophic diseases, there is already much we can do to start stretching out our years as much as possible.

Now, here's even better news. Some of things we can do to live longer are incredibly easy and inexpensive!

The Big Three Life Extenders

To ward off premature aging, increase your daily intake of vitamins C, E and A. Some upon reading this will balk, and say that it has never been conclusively proven that these three vitamins retard the aging process. That's true. On the other hand, there is a lot of compelling circumstantial evidence — and some evidence better than circumstantial — that these three vitamins do, in fact, slow the aging process. Furthermore, it is almost certainly harmless to increase your intake of each of these vitamin by some 200 percent. They are also relatively inexpensive. You don't even have to buy bottled supplements. Increasing your intake of foods that contain these high levels of these vitamins will have the same, if not better effect as bottled supplements.

While it is almost impossible to overdose on vitamin C (because it is essentially a food and your body processes it as such), large doses of vitamins E and A can produce toxic side effects in some people.

Because of the ease, availability and low cost of increasing your vitamin C, E and A intake, it is one of the best thing you can do right now to take a swat at the old Grim Reaper.

But there's more:

The Power of Friendship

That's right, there is strong scientific evidence to suggest that high levels of stress combined with lack of friends and family can significantly reduce your life span.

Scientists at the University of Goteborg in Sweden took a

random sample of 50-year-old men and gave them each a physical examination and psychological evaluation. Seven years later, the researchers went back to find the men, and also looked up those who had died. What they found was that, of the men who had died reported three or more recent upsetting events in their lives, 11 percent were dead. All of them identified themselves as lacking family or social support.

Of the men who had peaceful lives full of friends and family, just three percent had died.

The life events most strongly related to dying were having serious concerns about a family member, being forced to move, feelings of insecurity at work, serious financial trouble and being the target of legal action.

Swedish scientists think that stress may lower resistance to disease, and that lack of caring, loving people in your life provides less psychological "will" to fight off disease and to go forward with life.

Therefore, to significantly increase your chances of living longer, take a look at your own life. Do you have a family? a close friend or friends? If you don't, perhaps now is the time to open yourself up to the possibility. Now is the time to reach out to someone — after all, your life may depend on it!

(See entry under "acupressure" "meditation" "stress" and "color" for some excellent tips on reducing the effects of life-robbing stress).

Shed That Weight!

This one will be a bit tougher for many of you, but scientific studies have shown it to be tremendously effective in slowing the aging process. All evidence indicates that staying just below your normal weight will significantly increase your life span.

Those of you who already have weight problems are already groaning as you read this, I know. We can hear you. But it's our job to give you the facts. You are the one who has to act on them. And the facts say that staying just below the average weight for your size and body type will very probably make you live longer. Do you want to live longer? Then you'll have to shed that weight and get used to being just a tad hungry sometimes. Many people would say that starving and being hungry is not worth the trade-off for some extra years of life ... but that's something you'll have to come to terms with in your own mind.

Studies Prove That Meditation Keeps You Young

According to a study reported in the Journal of Behavioral Medicine, people who meditate on a regular basis have levels of age-related hormones that are comparable to those of meditaters five to 10 years younger.

A hormone with the $25 name of dehydroepaindosterone sulfate (DHEA-S) is produced by the adrenal gland. The rate at which it is produced normally increases through the early 20s, then begins to decline.

In the study, the level of DHEA-S of 423 meditators were compared to that of 1,252 health nonmeditators. The subjects were divided into groups according to their age, and meditators were compared to nonmeditators in the same age proximity.

Meditating females showed higher DHEA-S levels than nonmeditating women in every age group. Men under age 40 showed little variation, but after age 40, meditators began to show significantly higher levels of the youth hormone than nonmeditators.

(Note: Turn to heading under meditation elsewhere in this book to learn some simple meditation techniques you can start putting into practice today.)

Speaking of your mind, that brings us to perhaps the most powerful longevity advise we can give you:

Special Discussion on Aging: Mind Over Matter

Most advice in medical books and self help books will focus on the physiological factors or remedies that people can use to achieve longer life.   They try to adjust and manipulate the physical body as if it were a machine that could be made to run efficiently and perfectly forever if only the right ingredients can be found and added to it in the just the right amounts. But all the remedies and additives may be insignificant next to a few simple adjustments that you can make in your own mind.

Consider this:

What is your body made up of anyway?   Some of you might say: "Well, I've heard that the human body is about 90 percent water."   And you would be right.   But let's go beyond that.

Sure, your body is made up of water and various organic and inorganic molecules. Water is made up of molecules, too — H20, as you know.   Our bodies are made up of molecules, which in turn are made up of smaller particles called atoms, which in turn are made up of yet smaller subatomic particles, including protons, neutrons, electrons, quarks and so on.

As it turns out, scientists have discovered that these smaller subatomic particles are basically made up of nothing more than light-energy combined with ... nothing! Atoms are 99.999 percent empty space! Energy, in fact, is just "acting" like solid physical matter by being in many places at one time with great speed and the help of some other factors too difficult to explain here. But suffice it to say, your body, at its most fundamental level, is made up of pure light energy.

As Einstein told us, energy in the universe can never be destroyed, only transformed.

So if your body is made up of molecules, atoms and subatomic particles — which are actually whirling bits of light mixed with nothing — that makes you and your body a pretty remarkable thing! On a fundamental level, the energy which your body has is something that can never be destroyed, only transformed to a new or different level. That's a scientific fact!

Now, keep the above in mind while you consider this:

If you did not know how old you were, would you really be able to tell what your true age is? Don't be so sure!

Back before the Civil War days, most people did not know precisely how old they were. Just 150-some years ago, the general public was not as "time-obsessed" or age conscious as we are. Most people had a general idea about how old they were, but few knew — or cared — what their exact age was.

The result was that people did not expect certain life events to happen when a particular age was reached. "Manhood" was not automatically gained at age 18 or 21. People did not have a mid-life crises at age 35, or expect to die at age 72. How could they expect these things to happen if they had no idea about how old they were? A man in his fifties might guess his age at 40, or even 35 if he had no true idea about his age. Most likely, he would estimate his age based on how he felt. He felt young, vibrant and healthy, well, he would consider himself a man in the prime of his life — and his exact age would be a non-issue.

The point is that your age is far less of a solid, quantifiable and real thing than you have been lead to believe in our modern society, which is obsessed by time. In our modern world, each age comes with a label or expectancy. People in their eighties are assumed to be living on "borrowed time" because we expect people of that age to die at any time. People who reach the magic age of 65 are expected to retire, and we expect their health to begin a more rapid decline.

But if you didn't know you were 65 and you felt great and loved your job, why would you retire? You wouldn't. You would not let something as artificial as a birthday with some number attached to it effect your life.

So our experience of time is basically an illusion. It truly is. Now combine this fact with the fact that your body is made up of atoms and subatomic particles that are energy which can never be destroyed.

Are you starting to get the picture?

If you are not, this is it in a nutshell: That old saying, "You are as young as you feel" is far more true than you ever imagined. If time is truly an illusion, as we have showed, and if the substance of your body can never be destroyed, then you can easily live years and years longer if you just accept the reality of it.

There is no reason not to. Simply make a mental note in your mind that tells you that your age is nothing more than an artificial number, and that your body is a remarkable collection of super-charged energy that is in a perpetual state of existence in the universe.

The bottom line is: Aging is literally a state of mind. Why succumb to the artificiality of numbers? Instead, judge your personal age and longevity on something other than the pages of a calender. Re-set the inner clock of your mind to accommodate a life span of 130 years. With your mind leading the way, your physical body will follow. When you reach the age of 60 or 70, mentally consider yourself to be "middle aged" because you still have another 60 or 70 years to go. Try it and see. What have you got to lose?

Allergies

Well, no doubt, allergies have made a meteoric rise to fame and blame in both professional and popular medicine recently. Special "allergy clinics" and allergy specialists (allergists) are popping up all over the country. Allergies are being blamed for everything from migraine headaches to sexual disfunction.

Allergy clinics are cashing in big time from people who think they are suffering from some kind of allergy or another. But before you open your wallet for the expensive treatment of modern medicine (many of which do not work), let's see what you can do to solve your allergy problems on your own.

How to recognize an allergy?

To say it in a nutshell: It sure ain't easy.

If you think you might be having an allergic reaction to something, what might it be? Because the choice could be among any number of several thousand of substances you come into contact with everyday, singling out one or a few things often requires a detective with the advanced acuteness of a Sherlock Holmes.

Even highly sophisticated doctors with the best medical equipment and testing procedures are often stumped, and worse, mislead by their tests. More and more people are walking around these days thinking they are allergic to this substance or that, when in fact, their symptoms may come from another condition entirely, including psychosomatic sources.

Many allergists today are claiming that mood swings, depression, hyperactivity, sudden anger, and much more are all caused by allergic reactions — yet many of those doctors have not had a single day of psychiatric or psychological training to their credit which would enable them to properly recognize psychological conditions.

Perhaps one of the best pieces of advice to those who are nursing a half-dozens allergies these days would be to step back and take a second look. Modern medicine's new love-affair with allergies could be as much a fad as real science. An honest self assessment and a personal examination of your own perceived physical reactions may result in the abandonment of most of your allergies.

Sometimes it's easier to blame your uncomfortable emotions on a physical reaction or allergy, rather than face the real cause of your anger or depression.

Real Allergies

Acknowledging what we've said about the potential of imaginary allergies, let's go on and discuss the legitimate, physically-generated allergies that clearly do exist. No one can deny the timely onslaught of dusts and pollens in the spring and summer which send many people into miserable paroxysms of runny noses, swollen eyes, uncontrolled sneezing, skin rashes and scratchy or swollen throats. Pet dander and many common foods are also frequent culprits.

First of all, how do you know your sniffling and sneezing is caused by an allergic reaction and not a cold or something else?

Well, it's often just a matter of common sense. Colds and flu usually clear up within a week or so. An allergy comes and goes more frequently; unlike a cold, allergy symptoms can cease suddenly; allergies are more persistent and bother an individual over long periods of time; cold and flu usually come with fever and "sick all over" feelings, unlike allergies, which come with just the sneezing and swelling and runny noses.

Remember, though, that allegies can manifest themselves in your body in a variety of ways that go well beyond the typical sniffling, congestion and sneezing.

One of the best ways to find out what's triggering your allergic reaction is to pay attention! When you began to react, and you suspect it is an allergic reaction, stop a minute and take an inventory of where you are, what you have come into contact with, and what you have eaten.

Always consider the possibility that your allergic reaction could be something you have just eaten, or something you have just come into contact with in the environment. Connecting an allergy with a food can be as easy as writing down everything you eat, and watching yourself for signs of reaction. Often times, though, your reaction may be to a hidden ingredient within a food, rather than the food itself.

As an example of how insidious this can be, consider the case of a woman's reaction to chewing gum. The woman sought an allergist's help for a skin reaction caused by an inflammation of her blood vessels. After a battery of tests, it was found she was reacting to the common food preservative, BHT (butylated hydroxytoluene). BHT is added to everything from bread to chewing gum ...which is what caused the above woman's allergic reaction.

Food dyes, preservatives, food texurizing agents can all be culprits in producing your allergy. Once you think you have zeroed in on specific food, read the ingredient label and become familiar with every substance in the food. With enough detective work, you may be able to isolate what is tripping your allergy trigger.

What to do about allergies

Once you feel you have successfully identified a substance you are allergic to, the best plan of action is to avoid that substance at all costs.

While it's difficult to always avoid all-pervasive substance swhich float in the air — such as dust and pollen — there is much you can do to create a "safe place" for yourself when your allergies get really troublesome.

"Climatize" your house — Make your home or apartment inhospitable to dusts, molds and pollens. Take steps to eliminate high humidity in your home to suppress the growth of molds. Maintain temperatures at 70 degrees Fahrenheit or lower. Buy an air conditioner and an air cleaner to scrub the atmosphere inside your house, and avoid doing anything that will cause the air move around a lot, which help allergens spread. Think hard about where hidden molds can grow — the key will usually be moisture. Check your basement for access moisture, under the sink, all points in the bathroom, beneath carpets, and so on.

Move — Maybe you shouldn't let your allergies imprison you. If you are a truly implacable sufferer from allergies, you may want to consider moving to a part of the country that is more conducive to your health. Perhaps the dry air of a desert climate, like New Mexico? Or maybe the brisk northern states are less hospitable to the kinds of organic substances which set you off. This is a bit extreme, but sometimes moving for the sake of an allergy or good health can have an overall positive affect on your life. You may find a new job, new friends, and a heavenly, allergy-free environment.

Acupressure treatment — Two acupressure points are effective is reducing the symptoms of allergies. One is behind the knee, half way along the crease of the joint. The second is actually two points of either side of your backbone. Massage vigorously an area three vertebras down from the base of your neck.

Use over-the-counter drugs — Why not? For the most part, they really work. You don't need to get a prescription from a doctor, and you can simply walk into any drug store or grocery store to get what you need. Be cautioned, however, that symptoms which are severe and persistent may eventually require professional help. Page 16

Hot drinks — You don't have to be a rocket scientist to understand how hot, steamy liquids can provide relief to blocked nasal passages, puffy eyes and swollen throats. Some reports say that hot herbal tea is not a good choice to relieve an asthma attack because herbs themselves can trigger an allergic reaction! But the fact is, most people require many cups of a particular herb tea over a long period of time before an allergy will show itself to the product. Some studies also suggest coffee is the best hot drink to use to stop an allergic reaction because of the anti-allergy effect of the caffeine it contains. But remember, each cup of coffee contains from 75 to 110 milligrams of caffeine. Since a mere glass of cola — which contains about 25 mg of caffeine — can send some people into a nervous dither, you may not know whether you are having an increased allergic reaction, or a caffeine reaction. So stick with hot water, or hot decaffeinated coffee or tea,(which usually contains about 2 mg of caffeine).

A hot shower is tremendous — When your sinuses are blocked and breathing is becoming incredibly difficult, get in a hot shower and let the water hit your face. You will not only feel great relief, but your sinuses will respond quickly by shrinking down.

Mind over Matter A special allergy discussion:

Consider this true story:

A psychiatrist was treating a patient with multiple personality disorder (sometimes known as "split personality"). The patient manifested four or five different personalities — one was an old man, another a young boy, one a female, and so on. Health care workers noted on the man's admission that he had a life-long, severe allergy to orange juice. Just a sip instantly raised angry red hives on the patient's skin, and also made him very sick and irritable.

On one occasion, however, the patient was accidentally given orange juice while in his "little boy" personality. The result? No allergic reaction. Even though each personality occupied the very same physical body, only one was allergic to orange juice.

How could this be? Well, this case clearly shows that an allergy is not always a physiological problem. In fact, some researchers have used hypnotism to demonstrate that allergies are far more "in the head" than they are physical problems. In the experiments with hypnotism, many people were given substances they had been long allergic to while being given the hypnotic suggestion that they were drinking only pure water. The result? No allergic reaction.

We have provided this information on allergies not to suggest that all of your allergies are "in your head," or to suggest you are having some kind of emotional problem that you are blaming on an allergy. Perhaps you actually do have a physical intolerance to a particular food or substance. But the above examples should at least give you reason to pause, and take a closer look at what is going on with your body.

Alzheimer's and Senility

After all these years and after all the millions of people, mostly elderly, that have suffered from loss of their mental faculties and control of their bodies, the mystery of Alzheimer's Disease and senility is just that — a mystery.

The best evidence now points to aluminum as the probable culprit for Alzheimer's Disease. But before we get into that, is there any difference, you might ask, between Alzheimer's and just "plain old senility?"

That's a difficult question to answer. Alzheimer's, which was once called "senile dementia" is extremely difficult to diagnose, even by experienced doctors who have studied the problem for years. Symptoms of senility can be caused by a large number of problems. Some of them are:

• Nutritional and vitamin deficiencies
• Too many medication, or the wrong kind of medications
• Strokes
• Psychological factors
• Low thyroid function

- Brain tumors
- A blow to the head
- Infections such as venereal disease or Lymes Disease

And others. Morbidly, positive identification of Alzheimer's is only possible after a person has died and the brain has been examined. People with Alzheimer's show a minute amount of aluminum at the center of each nerve cell in the brain.

It has been shown that aluminum inhibits the formation of a brain chemical called choline esterase, which is needed to maintain proper functioning of the brain.

The moral of the story is that avoiding aluminum in our food, drinks and environment early in life may prevent senility or Alzheimer's from ever striking you later in life. The section in the book under "Hidden Toxins in Your Life" give extensive information about aluminum and how to avoid it in your food and environment.

Try zinc

As for what you can do about Alzheimer's, the options are not many and not very effective. There is some evidence to suggest that increasing the intake of zinc will counter the effects of the aluminum in the brain which is causing the problem. But before you go out and give your Alzheimer's patient large amount of zinc supplements, be warned that too much of any one metal in your body, whether it be iron, copper or other trace elements, can set all your dietary metals off balance.

Lecithin and choline

Another possible remedy for Alzheimer's is lecithin, a complex body fat present in high concentration in the brain and nerves. Lecithin mixed with Choline, which is part of vitamin B complex, are what help make up choline esterase, which the brain needs to function properly.

You can buy both lecithin and choline supplements in health food stores and adding them to the diet of people with Alzheimer's may improve their condition, but don't expect miracles.

An ordinary aspirin a day

Senility is often associated with a number of small strokes that have caused brain damage and senility. Aspirin will help thin the blood and prevent further blockages and strokes, and may improve brain function by allowing more blood and oxygen into the brain.

A little compassion goes a long way

Always remember that the dementia and personality problems that can result from Alzheimer's and similar diseases are not the fault of the individual. They need your love and support more now than ever. Treating such people with tremendous patience and kindness will go a long way towards making everyone's life a bit easier.

Remember ...

It can't be stressed enough that Alzheimer's disease is frequently misdiagnosed! And that could be good news for your loved one. Perhaps the problem is not as bad as you think. Make sure you make a careful evaluation of the medications the person is taking, or look closely into the diet and nutritional history of the person. Sometimes clearing up senility is simply a matter of reducing medications, or supplementing the diet with badly needed nutritional supplements. Check out all the possibilities before you give up hope. With a little luck, the answer to senility may be a simple one.

Anal Fissures

The words anal fissure sounds like a rather unpleasant subject for conversation. But if you want unpleasant, develop an anal fissure of your own and you'll really have something to complain about.

A fissure is just a fancy word for a crack in the skin. Just as the skin on your hands or face can become cracked due to dryness, the skin around your rectum can tear and crack, and result in problems very similar, if not the same, as hemorrhoids.

Cause and prevention are linked

Perhaps the biggest cause of anal fissures are stools that are too hard. Hard stool results from a low-fiber diet. Too much meat, fat, white bread and pastries, cheese and so on will harden your stools, which may then tear and crack the skin around the you-know-what. Starting today, include beans, wheat bran, rice, corn, bulgar and whole wheat bread in your daily diet — at least once a day. This will aid your digestion, soften your stool and give your bottom a chance to heal.

Vitamins A and D

You probably already know that vitamin's A and D are very important to maintaining healthy skin. Well, most drug or department stores stock what is called "A & D Ointment" on their shelves. This is a product similar to petrolium jelly which contain vitamins A and D. Long-term care facilities, such as nursing homes, often use A & D to heal bed soares and other open skin wounds. Using it on your anal fissures will greatly speed healing.

Water instead of wiping

Common sense tells you that rubbing an open wound with a rough cloth will not feel good, and may not help. Most toilet paper can be too harsh for some of the worse anal fissures. If you can, use a warm water spray instead of wiping, then dab yourself dry. Also, taking a warm bath will help keep fissures clean, pliable and free of feces, which can cause burning and infection.

Use common sense

You already know what makes your bottom feel worse, that too much friction and rubbing is counter-productive, that being overweight puts more pressure on your bottom, and so forth. Treat yourself, and your behind, with a little TLC and give it a chance to catch up and heal up.

Anemia

You know what it means to say someone is "anemic." Many descriptive words immediately come to mind: weakness, pale skin, tiredness, feeling slow, groggy, cold, numbness, run down, fatigued, and more.

If you persistently feel one or all of these symptoms, you may be anemic. The only proper way to get a true diagnosis of anemia is to get a blood test. But once you have that, there is much you can do to fix the problem without a lot of expensive medical care.
Most often, anemia is caused by a nutritional deficiency that does not allow enough iron, vitamin B-12 and folic acid (folic acid is also a B vitamin) into your diet and blood stream. Surprisingly, anemia is more often a disease of youth and childhood than it is of old age.

Other common causes of anemia are excessive blood loss due to ulcers, cancer, heavy menstruation or other bleeding sources. Pregnancy is also commonly linked to anemia.

The most common kind of anemia is iron-deficient anemia and a way to deal with it is as follows:

Vitamin C

As it does with so many other diseases, the mighty vitamin C can greatly assist anemic people to have better iron absorption from their food to blood. Although vitamin C supplements are okay, it's best to get your C directly from foods rich in the substance. Here are best sources of vitamin C:

broccoli	brussels sprouts
cabbage	cantaloupe
cauliflower	collard greens
grapefruit	grapefruit juice
oranges	orange juice
pineapple	pineapple juice
spinach	strawberries

And many others, but the above have the highest concentration of vitamin C. Of course, many, many common fruits and vegetables have vitamin C and will be well worth including in your diet.

Add meat, fish and don't forget the legumes

Increasing your intake of vitamin C while also making sure you get small to moderate amounts of lean beef, poultry and fish (especially tuna) will add the iron to your diet that you need. Plentiful iron with vitamin C to help it integrate into the blood will be tremendously beneficial to anemic people. Remember, that an excellent source of non-meat iron are legumes of all kinds, including peas, peanuts, green beans and others.

Heavy on the almonds

Almonds are a superb source of iron. One cup of chopped, raw almonds contains 6.1 milligrams of iron. One cup of almonds provides you with 41 percent of the Recommended Dietary Allowance (RDA) of iron. Peanuts, pecans and roasted cashews are also pretty good sources of iron. Snack on them all day and you'll do wonders for your iron intake. Raisins are another superb source of iron and are as easy to pop as almonds.

Avoid tea and coffee

Studies show that coffee and tea can inhibit your body's ability to absorb iron if you drink it with a meal. Tea is especially inhibiting to iron absorption so you should avoid it.

Dairy products and eggs may reduce iron absorption

Some studies also show that milk, cheese, ice cream, and other dairy products may inhibit the absorption of iron into your body. Eggs have been identified as well. Reducing or eliminating most of these from your diet may improve your iron levels, and losing them will help you lose a lot of fat, cholesterol and sodium as well.

Don't forget to forget alcohol

Alcohol, which is almost so universally bad for our bodies, may also be a major contributor to other kinds of anemia in which the vitamins B-12 and folic acid are deficient. Drinking too much alcohol causes our bodies to lose vitamins of all kinds, both through the urine, and by breaking them down directly in our bodies. So your drinking problem may be creating even more of a problem in your life than you thought.

Iron Supplements

You can get iron supplements over the counter and they will most likely be necessary to get your body the iron it needs if you are anemic. See you doctor before you take them, however, because they can produce some unpleasant side effects, such a digestive disorders and dizziness.

Angina

Angina, often simply called "chest pains" can make a person feel like he or she is dying. The pain usually begins near the heart or stomach and can spread throughout the torso and neck.

What causes angina? Most medical experts agree that hardening and blocking of the arteries by cholesterol is the major culprit. What causes hardening of the arteries? You guessed it — too much of the wrong kind of fat (although some fats are good for you) in your diet.

Note: hardening of the arteries and cholesterol blockages are also known as a arteriosclerosis (hardening of the arteries) and atherosclerosis (hardening of the inner lining of the arteries).

Needless to say, the best way to fight angina (short of drugs and surgery for the worst cases) is to reduce the level of cholesterol in your blood, and to eat foods which can clean out arteries.

For a number of foods and anti-cholesterol agents, turn to the heading under "cholesterol in this book. Eating the foods and adding the supplements listed there will go a long way toward easing your angina.

Remember, also, that stress, too much physical exertion and strong emotions can trigger angina attacks. When that happens you need to take time out for a breather. (Don't take a cigarette break! That could kill you!) Calm yourself, relax, do something quiet and fun, but which does not require physical exertion.

Blocked arteries and high cholesterol levels can lead to heart attacks and heart disease. Getting started as early as possible on a low-cholesterol diet will not only ease your chest pains, but it will almost certainly add years to your life.

One final note: aspirin can help angina:

One aspirin tablet a day has been found to relieve and prevent attacks of angina by thinning the blood and rendering it less likely to clot. This not only eliminates the chest pain of angina, but also lowers your risk of other heart disease.

(Note: See heading under "Meditation" for some easy mind/body calming practices.)

Anorexia

The chronic inability to eat, or loss of desire to eat, has become a high-profile disease in the past two decades, perhaps because so many celebrities have died from this strange illness.

The victims of anorexia are usually young females with an overwhelming desire to be thin. Today, about one in 250 women suffer from anorexia and its causes are complex and psychological, often generating misunderstanding from people who can't understand why some people "just won't eat."

It's not as simple as that. If it were just a matter of "making someone eat" hundreds of people would not be dying from this illness every year.

Ironically, anorexia is closely associated with its very opposite — chronic overeating and obesity. Many people "binge and purge", i.e., they stuff themselves and then poke their finger down their throats to get rid of what they ate.

Perhaps the most important thing to remember about anorexia is that it is not simply a "poor appetite." It probably has little to do with appetite or food at all, and more likely is the result of a deep-seated psychological disorder that is manifesting itself in an inability to eat.

To treat anorexia, don't seek out a diet plan or try to stimulate yourself with enticing foods — to the anorexic, there are no enticing foods. Anorexia is a problem for a psychologist, not a dietician.

Most likely, the source of anorexia has something to do

with the psychological relationship between the victim and the victim's parent. That's not to say that the parent is "to blame" for the child's anorexia. But the source of the problem is often located in the relationship between mother and daughter, although many other possibilities should be studied.

If you can't search within yourself to find the psychological "trigger" of your anorexia, or if you suspect that the problem stems from somewhere within your familial relationships, seek the help of a psychologist, counselor or self-help group to assist you in finding the answers you need.

To start eating again, you need to remove the invisible mental block that stands between you and a normal life of food, family and friends. Get started today. The longer you let anorexia linger, the less likely you will be able to overcome it.

Anxiety
(Also, see "Stress")

These days our lives are filled with fears and dangers — big fears and little fears, big dangers and little ones. Many of them are entirely appropriate; they help us to stay out of trouble, or get ourselves out of tight situations.

For example, you should feel fear if you are walking by yourself down a dark street in a gang-infested neighborhood with no protection at your disposal beyond harsh language. Or suddenly your car goes out of control on an icy road and you begin to swerve toward the ditch or into oncoming traffic.

Panic! You have to react! Take quick action! But the result

will either be a safe resolution of the situation, or some level of disaster. Either way, the source of anxiety will be gone and you will deal with whatever comes next.
But not all sources of anxiety in our lives are so dramatic. There can be dozens of low-grade anxieties for us to face everyday, all of which can build up over time and trigger "anxiety attacks." Every day anxieties include the pressure of your job; a difficult relationship with significant other or children or parents; financial worries; freeway traffic; giving a speech and others.

You may also have specific fears of phobias, such as fear of heights or water or dogs.

Dealing effectively with anxiety is becoming more and more important today, since we have more of it in our lives.

Meditation

What could be cheaper, take less time, and work better than a daily session of meditation? Nothing we can think of. Just 10 minutes twice a day can completely free you of an inability to handle anxiety. You will never rid your life of all sources of fear, but a daily session of meditation will greatly increase your ability to handle them.

Don't be put off by some of the "exotic" or bizarre associations you may have about meditation. Not all meditation is connected to Eastern religions, cults or New Age practices. Meditation can be something as simple as sitting quietly in your chair for ten minutes, and just letting go of your thoughts while you concentrate on your breathing. That doesn't sound like much, but the power of quieting your mind and learning to breath a bit more deeply could make an astonishing change in your life. It could easily increase your power to "cope" by 100 percent or more.

For some specific meditation techniques, see the heading under "meditation" in this book.

Food and vitamins

Many foods, vitamins and specific amino acids help the biochemistry of your body fight off the effects of stress and anxiety. See the heading under "stress" in this book for more specifics about what these are.

Remember: "Crisis" is another word for "Opportunity"

The Chinese symbol for crisis is a combination of the characters of "danger" and "opportunity." In every anxiety producing situation lies a potential opportunity for growth and gain. It's how you handle the situation that makes all the difference. Your beliefs and expectations are what will drive the ultimate outcome. Try not to have a "fear-based" personality, but rather and "opportunity-based" personality.

How you think about a situation can make all the difference in the world. One person may hate thunderstorms, for example, because he or she is afraid of lightning and thunder, wind and hail. That person expects the worst, and may often find him/herself being confronted with the worst. Another person, on the other hand, may love thunderstorms because the beautiful display of "fireworks", because the rain is needed and because the air will be made fresh when it passes by.

A thunderstorm is a thunderstorm — but how you choose to experience it internally determines the true nature of its reality.

Arthritis

Did you know that there are more than 100 different kinds of arthritis?

Furthermore, each kind is extremely difficult to recognize and diagnose. Even the most experienced doctors struggle to identify the particular form of arthritis you might have. What's worse, finding the cause of your disease is even more difficult, if not impossible.

In general, medical researchers say there is "no known cause of this disease, and no known cure."

Even so, treating arthritis has not become a highly advanced science. Mainstream medicine has developed a vast array of drugs and therapies, all designed to battle arthritis, whether that treatment be pain reduction, slowing the progress of the disease, or surgically replacing joints and knuckles that have been twisted out of shape by this insidious disease.

As millions of arthritis sufferers know, many of the current treatments can be as bad as the disease itself. Side effects from the medicine, the ruinous financial costs of treatment and medicines, and all else associated with this painful affliction can devastate a person's life.

Yet despite all that is known about arthritis, despite all the research and advancement of mainstream science, and despite the general consensus that it can't be cured — many people do, in fact, find a cure for their arthritis.

Consider an example from Dr. William Crooks's book, The Yeast Connection. Crook tells of a woman who had been diagnosed by another physician with rheumatoid arthritis, and who had been prescribed standard arthritis medication.

Crook decided to add an antifungal medication, called nystatin, to her diet that would kill excess yeast cells in her intestinal tract. About a week after she began her arthritis medications, she was forced to quit because of severe skin rash the drugs produced.
After quitting the arthritis medicines, her health got better, not worse.

That's because the woman continued with the Antifungal medication, nystatin. Within a few weeks, her symptoms of arthritis began to disappear. Crook also instructed the woman to discontinue certain foods that "bothered" her — primarily foods that contained yeast, or yeast enhancing substances, such as sugar.

The final result was that the woman felt "100 percent better." Her arthritis, it seemed, had more to do with her diet and an intestinal yeast infection than it did with the famous "unknown causes" of those who traditionally treat arthritis.

Other people who have shown all the symptoms of arthritis have discovered allergic reactions to certain foods or environmental substances. Others have experienced spontaneous remission of their symptoms, while still others have found that mega-vitamin and "deep massage" therapy have helped far more than traditional medicine. The point is, you shouldn't settle only for your doctor's say-so when it comes to arthritis. Be willing to explore new options to rid yourself of your pain and suffering.

Now, here are some tips and advise on where you can start your personal search for an arthritis "cure."

Look into the yeast-mold-allergy connection

Your arthritis may have a lot to do with a poor diet, and a

proliferation of yeast cells in your digestive system. Yeast cells occur naturally in your intestinal tract, but sometimes antibiotic drugs, a diet of too many sweets, breads, meats and mold-bearing foods can produce an overpopulation of yeast cells in your body. The result is a lot of toxic secretions by the cells into your bloodstream, resulting in many adverse effects, including arthritis.

One of the best natural "yeast cell killers" is garlic. If you dramatically increase your garlic intake — say by one or two cloves per day — you may notice beneficial effects within a couple of weeks. You can also buy easy to take garlic supplements at any drug store or supermarket.

Garlic, in general, has long been used for its beneficial effects on inflammation and arthritis. Give garlic a try. At worst, it is a nutritional food that will be a positive supplement to your overall diet.

Give up sweets

For one thing, sweets are a primary food for yeast cells. Avoiding sweets, breads (which contain yeast) too much meat and mold-bearing foods will help cleanse your body of toxins and starve yeast cells. Sweets in general, especially white sugar, have long been suspects in aggravating arthritis. Even if it does not help your arthritis, giving up sweets will be beneficial for many other reasons, from weight control to improving your overall diet.

Give up coffee

Coffee is one of the worst substances for people with arthritis. First, it has a high level of acidity which can help break down cartilage in joints and contribute to the advancement of arthritis. Caffeine contributes to stress and nervousness — both major culprits in increasing the pain and progress of arthritis. There are also many other oils and substances in coffee that are believed to worsen arthritis symptoms. In short, if you have arthritis, coffee is one of the worst things you can give it.

Try a low-fat diet

The connection between diet and arthritis has long been controversial. For many years The Arthritis Foundation has dismissed any connection between diet and arthritis. One of the Foundations pamphlet reads: "The possible relationship between diet and arthritis has been thoroughly and scientifically studied ... the simple proven fact is that no food has anything to do with causing arthritis and no food is effective in treating it."

But we're sorry, Arthritis Foundation — you are clearly wrong about this one. The fact is, many people have discovered real relief by switching to a diet low in fat, and high in fiber and vitamin. According to the book, Arthritis Relief, by Jean Wallace, many new studies show that a low-fat diet can have a significant effect on relieving arthritis symptoms.

Doctors at the University of Florida, for example, have found that certain foods, such as dairy products and shrimp, trigger flair-ups in a small amount of sensitive people. An improved, leaner diet with little or no meat has helped a large number of people to significantly reduce inflammation, and relieve the fatigue associated with arthritis. You really owe it to yourself to try a low-fat diet for several months. You have nothing to lose but a lot of fat and cholesterol, and you may gain a upper hand against the persistent and insidious disease of arthritis.

Avoid milk

Still on the diet note, a lot evidence suggests that milk may be the culprit behind many people's affliction of rheumatoid arthritis. This includes food such as cookies and cakes, which may contain milk as an ingredient. Stop drinking milk for a couple of months and see what happens.

Eat more fish

There is now solid evidence that certain fish oils may suppress symptoms of arthritis. The fish oil identified with helping arthritis is omega-3, and is found in freshwater fish, especially salmon. Omega-3 supplements are also available in health food stores, but taking these is less effective and less desirable than getting your omega-3 directly from the source. Fish oil tablets may cause belching or loose stools.

Some other allergy?

Your arthritis may be the result of another food entirely. Everyone is different, and you may have a specific allergy to a specific food. Identifying such a food is not easy. Perhaps the best idea is to keep a journal of your symptoms, keeping a close eye on your level of pain and inflammation, and then trying to match it up with something you have eaten recently. Once you think you have found something that makes your pain worse, avoid that food for several weeks, then try it again as a test. If your body reacts negatively, then you may have isolated something that is giving you trouble.

Give these natural herbs a try

All of these herbs and special preparations have been identified with helping or healing arthritis. You can find all of these herbs in your health food store. Search them out and try them out for at least three months:

Devil's Claw   Tumeric
Bilberry   Hawthorne

Bromelain
Burdock Root
Sarsaparilla Root
Willow Bark

Hawthrone Berry
Yucca Powder
Ginger Root
Ginseng

Eat a lot more of these foods

Pineapple
Garlic
Herring
Onions

Pineapple juice
Brazil nuts
Salmon
Broccoli

Asthma

As many as 25 million people in America — about 1 in 10 people — suffer from some form of asthma. More than 4,000 people die from asthma every year.

The American Thoracic Society calls asthma an "episodic disease" which means if flares up from time to time, rather than causing every-day distress.

Asthma is caused by your air passageways becoming oversensitive to various environmental conditions. When an attack occurs, the airways swell and make if difficult to breath. It often corrects itself, but sometimes medication is needed to prevent serious harm to the asthma victim.

Asthma is more common in children than adults, and many children outgrow it. Yet, many people battle asthma all their lives.

Here are some natural ways you can battle your asthma attacks:

(1) Onions to the rescue. Onion extract on guinea pigs has

shown that it can be a major anti-asthma agent. Studies on humans have also shown that onion extract inhibited bronchial asthma. While you may not have a bottle of onion extract handy, try chewing on a slice of onion to treat your bronchial asthma attack.

(2) And once again, it's vitamin C to the rescue, at least for some people. Studies have shown that about one quarter of asthma suffers can relieve their symptoms with 500 mg of vitamin C. This is not a quick solution, but it will shrink the air passageway sooner.

(3) Climatize your environment and avoid those foods that may trigger you. Many asthma attacks are associated with allergies. If that's the case, you are likely already aware of the places, conditions and foods that make asthma attacks likely. See the "climatize" section under the "Allergies" heading in this book.

(4) Check your reaction to aspirin and aspirin-like drugs. These can be a major source of asthma attacks. Indomethicin, which is commonly used as an anti inflammatory for arthritis and others conditions, is also a likely asthma culprit. If you react to them, avoid them and use aspirin substitutes.

(5) Monitor your lifestyle changes. Your asthma condition will change if there's a change in your lifestyle due to environmental factors. Or, you may develop an intolerance to a certain drug or a sensitivity to a new substance. If you are taking any medications, tell your doctor or pharmacist about any asthma attacks you think may be associated with the drug.

(6) Remember, emotional stress can trigger asthma attacks. If that the case, maybe it's time for a "time out" and to find a quiet place to sit or lie down for a minute.

Some Breathing Tips for Asthmatics

(1) Try breathing through your nose when cold or windy weather leaves you breathless. This makes air moist and easier on the air passages.

(2) Wrap a scarf or muffler around your nose and mouth to retain moisture in cold dry weather.

(3) Avoid dry air and overheating your home. Warm, humid air leads to less asthma attacks. Woods stoves and fireplaces really dry out the air, so avoid these if you can. Too humid is no good either.

(4) Try pursed lip breathing. Do it this way: Close your mouth and inhale through your nose. Purse your lips and exhale slowly through your nose. Count as you exhale; exhale for twice as long as you inhale.

(5) Don't breath too hard or fast—that may lead to more airway constriction.

(6) Don't hold your breath between inhaling and exhaling

(7) Stop if the pursed lip exercise makes you dizzy or lightheaded.

Other asthma tips:

Coffee has been shown to help asthma attacks because of the shrinking effects provided by caffeine. Over-the-counter asthma products can be very effective take advantage of them!

Bad Breath (Halitosis)

Since way back in the 1700s, coffee has been hailed as an excellent remedy for bad breath. In fact, in The Dispensatory of the United States, published in 1868, coffee is credited with being able to get rid of "offensive and noxious effluvia from decomposing animal and vegetable substances."

But your common sense probably tells you that coffee can cause as much bad breath as it cures — if any.

Brush and Floss

The old Dispensatory is right about one thing though — stuff caught between your teeth can be a major source of bad breath. Always make sure your teeth are brushed and flossed and you will eliminate the odor of decaying food substances in your mouth.

Decaying teeth or gums is another matter, however. A rotten tooth could be the source of your bad breath, so you will need a dentist to deal with that. Ditto for problems with your gums, although there is much you can do about gum disease on your own. (See heading under "Dental Problems").

Eat that parsley

You thought that sprig of parsley on your plate was just for show? Well, there's more to it than that, Halitosis Head. Parsley is not just something to make your plate look good. Tradition has it that parsley is an excellent breath cleanser, especially to counteract the effects of onions and garlic. Many garlic supplements are pre-combined with parsley to eliminate the odor of garlic while retaining its benefits.

Fasting, dieting and low moisture

If you have ever tried fasting you've probably noticed that your mouth gets dry and sticky and that you may develop bad breath. Some say the smell is from toxics being eliminated from your body as you fast and cleanse your system. Whatever the reason, fasting, dieting can lead to a dry mouth which tends to give off an odor, toxins or no toxins. Rinse out your mouth with water, or brush with some baking soda. That should take care of it.

Diseases

Many serious, chronic or hidden diseases can cause bad breath. If your bad breath doesn't seem to be caused by any of the obvious things, consult a doctor about some other condition that may be producing this effect.

Back Pain

What do a snake, a corpse and an insect have in common?

They're all disgusting things? Well, yes, but when it comes to lower back pain, these exercise positions from the tradition of Yoga may be just what you need for relief. They are called the Corpse, the Cobra and the Locust.

In fact doing these exercises daily may leave you completely free of all back pain.

I suppose we could expend a few more paragraphs talking about how and why these exercises work, but let's get right to them instead. You can return to your reading after your back pain is gone!

Preparation

First find a place and a time of day where you will not be disturbed for about 20 minutes. You can do this in your office or at home, but make sure you have some privacy and that you will not be disturbed. Wear loose-fitting clothes and prepare a soft, but firm place for yourself on the floor. A blanket or a mat on the carpet should do nicely.

The Cobra

(1) Lie flat on your stomach, hands by your side, feet together.

(2) Place your hands, palms down, beside your waist, fingers pointing forward.

(3) Inhale and begin lifting yourself up on your hands, bringing the head back and arching the spine as far as it will go. Keep your legs straight. Don't bend your knees — you want to lift yourself up sort of as if you were doing a push-up if your legs were paralyzed. (Your're sort of doing an imitation of a Cobra).

(4) The arms don't need to be completely straight, but keep your pubic area firmly pressed to the floor.

(5) Exhale. Bend the knees and now attempt to bring the toes to the back of the head.

(6) Hold the pose there for about 15 seconds if you can while you breath in and out normally.

(7) Relax and repeat again.

The Corpse

(1) Lie flat on your back with your arms at your sides.

(2) Slowly stretch out your arms from your sides to above your head and stretch your entire body while taking a slow, deep breath, sucking in your stomach. Keep your mind clear and concentrate on your breathing only.

(3)Slowly put your arms back down to your sides as you exhale, and feel your entire body relax.

The Locust

(1) Lie on your stomach, hands by your side, palms up.

(2) Raise your head and place the front of the chin only on the floor.

(3) Make fists of your hands and place them under the thighs in the groin.

(4) Inhale, stiffen the body and push down on your arms. Bring the legs up in back as high as they will go.

(5) Hold the pose for 15 seconds or as long as you can while holding your breath.

(6) Exhale and lower your legs. Relax.

A simple back pain position that will help

Here's an exercise that could be better described as a position than a real exercise, but it has proven beneficial for many people and its very simple:

Lie on your back and put your lower legs up on a chair. Your knees should point directly up at the ceiling. Your back and spine should be straight and be firmly flat on floor. That's all there is too it. Maintain this position for about 30 minutes, while you clear your mind and breath deeply, but simply. Assume this position several times a day for shorter periods of time if you wish. Try it out whenever your lower back pain starts to act up. It should provide you with great relief.

Some further back pain tips

Don't perform any of the above exercise if they increase your back pain. Be careful. When doing the Cobra, lift your head and spine slowly, as if a chain that you were lifting one link at a time.

Bitter Herbs - Major Benefits

What may be bitter and unpleasant to swallow, may also be a source for a major improvement in your health.

In centuries past, a spoonful of "bitters" every morning for both children and adults was thought to be an excellent prevention against diseases of all sorts, especially stomach and intestinal sicknesses, and many others.

Bitters are any number of spices, herbs, plants or distillations that have an acidic or bitter taste. You're all familiar with common bitters, such as vinegar, garlic, ginger, red pepper, even coffee or tea. But there are literally dozens of other, lesser known herbs that, although bitter to the taste, offer major benefits to your health

Today, it is generally thought that an herb with a bitter taste indicates the presence of certain alkaloids which nuetralize toxic acids in your body.

Bitter herbs are believed to:

* Cleanse the blood

* Reduce cholesterol

* Act as an anti-biotic, and also kill viruses and parasites

* Balance the acidic level of the blood

* Improve digestion and enhance appetite

In important thing to remember about taking bitters for improving health is that, dosages that are too large will cause ill effects. But bitters taken in very small amounts will provide all of the benefits listed above.

So which bitter herbs work the best, and how do you go about taking them. Here's a recipe from the book Way of Herbs by Michael Tierra.

Combine the powders of the following:

6 parts gentian root
6 parts goldenseal
4 parts echinacea root
4 parts calamus root
2 parts myrrh
2 parts dandelion root
2 parts centaury root
2 parts wormwood
2 parts anise seed
1 part ginger root
1 part licorice root

Then add four ounces of powdered preparations of these herbs (which can be found in any health food store, or by consulting a herbalists guide or catalog) with a quart of vodka (yes, vodka) in a covered container. Allow this to steep for two weeks before straining for use.

Alcohol is a long-standing base ingredient for herbal preparations. Don't use rubbing or isopropal alcohol. A pharmaceutical-approved alcohol is best, but using an easy bottle of vodka or gin is just as effective and cheaper. Alcohol in minute amounts is a safe, medically effective medium which suspends active ingredients and assists in maintaining a microbe-free environment for your bitters.

Now that you have your bitter herb concoction, store in a small bottle, preferably with an eye dropper. Put 10 to 30 drops of the mixture under your tongue every morning to obtain the optimum benefits of your bitters preparation.

Your herb mixture can also be used in special circumstances, such as to treat diarrhea, or to treat inflammatory conditions, such as gout and arthritis. You can also take your mixture before or after meals to aid in digestion and to prevent gas or bloating.

Especially here in America, our diet is lacking in bitter flavors. Adding these bitters to your daily diet may have far reaching, beneficial effects on your health. Give it a try! You have everything to gain, and you may learn a lot more about the healing power of herbs in the process of finding and gathering these herbs, and putting them to use for your improved health.

Bladder Problems

Bladder problems ... well there are all kinds and many causes. The kind that you specifically have may be something of a challenge. Seek help from a doctor if you have to.

Bladder trouble, or more specifically, incontinence, belongs primarily to the realm of youths under the age of 16 or elderly people, mostly in long-term care facilities. Incontinence, or the inability to properly hold your urine, has several different causes — from blocked tubes, to weak muscles, or plain old stress.

Another common bladder problem is bladder infection, most frequently experienced by women. Let's look at bladder infections first.

Cystitis

Also known as cystitis, bladder infections are believed to be caused by the bacteria E. coli, a germ found in stool. Cystitis commonly attacks young, recently married women, and sexual intercourse is a common cause. Women may also suffer from cystitis after a vaginal infection.

Cystitis in men may result from an enlarged prostate, a narrowing of the urethra.

Symptoms are a burning during urination, chills, fever, increased urination, pain in the pubic area, backache, blood in the urine and urethral or vaginal discharge.

What to do about cystitis

Bed rest is important, especially if fever is involved. Increase your intake of liquids to help wash out the urinary tract. Take aspirin, which has an analgesic effect on the pain. Take long baths, and avoid alcohol, tea and coffee during the illness because they irritate the urinary tract.

The French Flush — preventing cystitis

Women who have frequent cystitis are often found to be habitually low on liquid intake. Because of this, European doctors commonly recommend the "French Flush" — drink two large glasses of water after intercourse to clean out the tubes.

Cystitis often requires the help of a doctor, so if pain, fever and other symptoms persist for more than a day, see a doctor.

Incontinence

The other common bladder problem is incontinence, or an inability to hold in your urine properly — dribbling, leaking, bed wetting and so on. Most often a problem for elderly people, this can have tremendous psychological implications and can make people "ashamed." The result is that most try to hide the problem, which only makes it worse. Seeing a doctor or taking steps to deal with incontinence can be very effective with a majority of cases.

Exercise you r muscles

You can greatly increase control over your bladder by exercising the muscles that control urine retention and flow. They're easy to locate. The next time you urinate, stop yourself in midstream. This action flexes the muscles you want to strengthen. By contracting these muscles and holding them (whether you are urinating or not) for 3 to 5 seconds and then releasing them, you will be exercising them like you would any other muscle in your body. The same goes for stopping or holding back your bowel movement — using those muscles exercises them to make them stronger.

An exercise regimen, called Kegel exercises, calls for a person to perform the muscle contractions for several minutes each day, several times a day. In less than five minutes you can perform a hundred or more contractions, and greatly increase your strength in this area. After a just a couple of weeks, you will probably notice a significant return of control over your bladder.

What to avoid

All of these things can be major contributors to your bladder problems:

coffee	chili peppers
soda	hot spices
alcohol	tomatoes
chocolate	cigarettes

Watch your fluids

Don't dehydrate yourself to avoid incontinence, but watching what you drink and when, can help you cut down on accidents. If you're taking a long trip in a car or on an airplane, for example, you may want to avoid too much drinking for a period before you go. You can also bring along soft pillows to sit on to lessen the vibrations or jolting of traveling, which could lead to accidents.

HIP has Help

For more information about incontinence, you can write to HIP (Help for Incontinent People), P.O. Box 544, Union, SC 29379.

Blood Pressure

Okay, you know the drill. The condition is high blood pressure. The primary causes: too much salt, too much alcohol, too much weight.

High blood pressure, also known as hypertension, has received no shortage of attention in the past couple of decades. Hypertension is the famous "Silent Killer" we hear so much about in the media. High blood pressure earned its nickname because your blood pressure may be elevated without you knowing it. You may feel all around fine and healthy, when in fact, a stroke or heart attack may be lurking just around the corner.

So you don't have to be a rocket scientist to know what you need to do to treat your own high blood pressure (assuming you have taken time to go to any drug store, clinic, or hospital for a free blood pressure check to determine that you actually have high blood pressure). You need to lose weight, cut salt out of your diet and lower your alcohol consumption.

But lets look a bit more closely at eliminating harmful substances from your diet because it's more tricky that you might think.

The Hidden Salt/sodium factor

It's one thing to put the salt shaker away, and avoid the obvious salty foods, such as potato chips and salted peanuts. But there are many food in your diet which you probably thought were — without question — safe and healthy.

What about, for example, a bowl of cereal with milk? A good choice for someone with high blood pressure?

No! Especially if the cereal is Cherrios, which has a sodium content higher than many snack foods, including potato chips! Even the milk itself has a high level of natural sodium. In fact, milk and many kinds of cheese are extremely high in sodium and should be one of the first things restricted from a diet adjusted for hypertension.

Other cereals contain a similar level of sodium to Cherrios , so make sure you read the ingredient label carefully. Speaking of reading labels, those seeking to avoid excess salt in their diets should read all food labels. Remember that ingredients listed as Na, MSG sodium citrate and nitrates are all equally important to avoid.

So do your homework! Check those labels and don't assume that foods are okay simply because they don't taste salty.

But a hypertension diet is not all about avoidance and bland food. Two substances in particular have been show to dramatically reduce high blood pressure: potassium and calcium. Increasing your intake of potassium and calcium may help you defeat your battle with hypertension, so here are the foods which are highest in both:

Potassium

Apricots (dried)	beet greens
cantaloupe	cod
collard greens	cowpeas
dates	flounder
kidney beans	lentils
orange juice	parsnips
potatoes	prune juice
pumpkin seeds	rhubarb
salmon	scallops
soybeans	tuna

There are other food that contain potassium as well, but these are among the highest. Check a nutritional guide for other foods with potassium.

Calcium

Of course, milk is one of the best sources of calcium, but

for those with hypertension, milk has too much sodium to make this a good choice. No problem! Here are some other excellent food sources of calcium:

sardines with bones	bok choy
pink salmon with bones	mackerel
baked beans	okra
broccoli	tofu
mustard greens	

Note: Many antacid pills now contain calcium, but many also contain high amounts of sodium. Read the label!

The Alcohol Factor

It's long been known that too much drinking will lead to a stroke or heart attack sooner or later. So all of you heavy drinkers out there should just quit right now — and cold turkey is the best way. Right?

Well ... maybe, but it may not be that simple, or all that desirable, for that matter, to quit drinking cold turkey.

First, research shows that no alcohol in the diet may be less advantageous to reduced hypertension than one or two drinks per day.

Second, we all know that alcohol is an incredibly addictive drug. So to simply tell people with hypertension that they must stop all alcohol consumption immediately is unrealistic. If someone is already having more than two drinks a day, they may already have a serious addiction to alcohol, in which case, the problem goes well beyond hypertension. Even a strict two-beer-a-day-only drinker may find it exceedingly difficult to give up those couple of beers.

Quitting alcohol may very well be the most stressful for many people to do. Stress is a prime contributor to hypertension, so reducing alcohol consumption should be done carefully, and with the least stress as possible.

The bottom line is, each person needs to take a serious look at his/her daily alcohol consumption as it relates to high blood pressure. Because of the addictive nature of alcohol and enormous psychological factors that accompany any addiction, this will be a process that takes a lot of forethought, and a lot of serious self examination on behalf of thepatient and family.

Losing weight

Again, much the same as our discussion with alcohol, to simply command someone to lose weight for lower blood pressure is not a simple thing to do. You can't wave a magic wand that will automatically help you maintain a new diet — and even if you did, there is no guarantee it would work.

A lot of new revelations have been made in the area of weight loss recently, and the new consensus seems to be that "diets don't work!"

Perhaps that's true, perhaps not. For the sake of our discussion about hypertension, the key may be in those two lists of foods high in potassium and calcium.

Try adjusting your diet for, say, one month, with the emphasis on those foods high in potassium and calcium. In general, remember to eat more fruits and vegetables and less meat.

In fact, the "vegetarian connection" has become a well-recognized boon to those suffering from high blood pressure. Studies show that vegetarians have far, far less incidence of hypertension than do meat eaters.

So the bottom line on "the weight loss factor" is: don't worry so much about dieting, per say. Instead, favor those food high in calcium and potassium, and in general, eat more fruits and vegetables while moving to eliminate meat from your diet.

Meditate your Way to Lower Blood Pressure

As it does for so many other physical ailments, just a few minutes a day of quiet meditation has been shown — scientifically — to have an extremely beneficial effect on hypertension. See the heading under meditation in this book for a simple meditation technique you can put into practice right away.

Exercise

Of course, exercise is one of the most effective treatments for high blood pressure. It also helps in weight loss, improved circulation of the blood and oxygenates your entire system. But stay away from weight-lifting or isometric exercises. You've seen those pictures of Sylvester Stalone with building muscles and veins popping through his skin? Well, Stalone suffered from high blood pressure, and his weight lifting has been a big contributor.

Boils

Ugly, painful boils are the result of infection. Specifically, it is a bacteria called staphylococcus, which gets under your skin where they cause infections in glands and hair follicles. The swelling and fluids that fill boils are the body's defenses in action. Pus is the build-up of white blood cells which have been sent to the sight to fight off the staph germs.

Compress is best solution

Boils are best treated by applying a warm wash cloth or hot water bottle to the site three or four times a day. Do it until the boil breaks, or is re-absorbed into the body. If you want, you can try to drain the boil by nicking it (carefully) with a sterilized needle. Be careful not to poke the needle in deeply — just a nick will do.

Boils are rarely dangerous, but are painful, unsanitary and can spread. The best way to prevent them is to always maintain a good hand-washing regimen, preferably with a anti-bacterial soap. When it comes to the prevention of boils, cleanliness is truly next to godliness.

Mud Method

Some claim that warm mud pasted over a boil will help it dry up faster. Try it if you like, but it's probably a better idea to stay with a clean, warm compress. It will have the same affect as warm, moist mud. Applying mud or other substances may increase chance of infection, especially if the boil breaks.

Bronchitis

When you have a cough that soon becomes worse than an ordinary cough, and also involves difficulty in breathing and lots of mucus in your throat and lungs, then you probably have bronchitis, which is the swelling of your bronchial tubes.

Bronchitis is usually caused by bacterial or viral infections of the lower windpipe. It can be occasional, or repeat and become chronic. Oftentimes, bronchitis is the result of a cold or some other upper respiratory infection that has not been cleared up. Bronchitis is especially common among smokers.

Also associated with bronchitis is a sticky mucus, which is the by-products of your body's defense system building up in your lungs and bronchial tubes. Coughing is your body's attempt to clean out the extra phlem.

Here's What You Can Do To Help Yourself

(1) At first, you may not want to suppress your cough because it will help eject mucus from your lungs and bronchial tubes.

(2) Avoid breathing tobacco smoke, or avoid smoking at least until symptoms discontinue.

(3) Bed rest will really help. Remember, in the case of bronchitis, your body is fighting an infection and bed rest will conserve the energy of your body for healing.

(4) Drink all the liquids you can handle — it will loosen up the stickiness of your mucus and enable it to clear easier.

(5) Steam inhalation is helpful.

(6) A massage of the chest and back will help clear up the chest, aid in relaxation and increase blood flow to your lungs to help them battle the infection.

(7) Some studies show that red pepper and other hot spices help ease the effects of bronchitis. Try a spicy taco or Cajon or curried food and see if it helps.

Remember, bronchitis can lead to more serious lung diseases if you let it go too long. Some 45,000 people die every year from obstructive lung diseases — don't let your bronchitis get that far. See a doctor if you cough up blood, have severe chest pains, have a high fever, or if your condition persists for several days.

Bursitis

What is it? It's inflammation of the bursa, of course. What's a bursa? Well, to put it simply, it's a favorite spot on your shoulder, that is, the spot you have been using the most recently. The elbow is also associated with bursitis.
Bursitis mostly affects weekend athletes or people with desk jobs who spend a Saturday doing some manual labor around the yard or house. But it doesn't have to be hard labor or heavy lifting that brings on bursitis. You can get it from too much Nintendo, or from bowling. To put it simply, bursitis is overuse of the shoulder or elbow. Depending on what you were doing, what motion you were using, and what part of the shoulder or elbow you were using, inflammation of the soft tissue may result and you will have pain, stiffness and possibly an accumulation of fluid in the joint.

You may notice visible swelling, and sometimes even slight movement will cause great pain.

Beating Bursitis

(1) The best way to beat it is to do the opposite of what caused it — nothing. That is, you should completely rest your shoulder or elbow on a pillow and avoid all possible use. Wear a sling if you have to, but the more rest you give your shoulder, the greater chance it will have to heal

up. (Note: This doesn't mean you should let your muscles atrophy for two weeks! Take a couple of days, then start normal use again — but avoid the particular motion you think may have caused the inflammation to begin with.)

(2) Put some ice on it. A cold compress or ice will bring the swelling down, especially early after inflammation ensues.

(3) Aspirin is one of the best anti-inflammatory drugs around. If you have no other problems taking aspirins (such as asthma or stomach problems) aspirins will really help.

(4) After swelling has gone down, a heating pad may be helpful, but discontinue if swelling comes back.

Get a massage

After your pain is gone and you think you're back to normal, you may want to massage your shoulders to limber and tone them up to prevent further occurrences of bursitis. Also, remember to give your body a warm up before you put strain on any part. This will ease you into the physical work or exercise and will go a long toward preventing injury from overuse.

Cancer

Do you want to cut your chances of getting cancer by 50 to 100 percent — starting today? You can! And you don't need a lot of money, undergo any expensive, high tech medical treatments, or buy any pricey vitamin supplements.

More than ever, cancer specialists are getting excited over the tremendous power of diet to prevent cancer, and help those with cancer to overcome their illness.

To dramatically reduce your risk of developing cancer is increase your daily intake of a number of common foods, as well as search out a few lesser known vegetables that contain super cancer-fighting agents.

First, lets discuss the common foods that have shown tremendous ability to prevent people from getting cancer.

The cruciferous vegetables

These vegetables are called "cruciferous" because they belong to a group of plants that generally have a four-petaled flower which suggests the shape of a cross.

As it turns out, the connections may be very appropriate. Many associate Christianity with the power of healing, and crucifeous plants may possess that ability as well.

The most common cruciferous plants are broccoli, cabbage, brussels sprouts, kale, mustard greens, collard greensl, turnips and others. Without a doubt, the No. 1 cancer fighting vegetable is ... drum roll please — broccoli!

Yes, former President Bush made big news by proclaiming his dislike for the famous bunched green vegetable, but in eschewing broccoli from his diet, the former President gave up a major weapon against one of our most deadly diseases.

Broccoli fights cancer in many ways. It is rich in carotene, a major anticancer agent. It is high in vitamin C and calcium, two more major cancer fighters. It contains almost no fat, but does have fiber and loads of potassium. As you will recall from reading our section under blood pressure control, calcium and potassium are major remedies for reducing high blood pressure.

The rest of the cruciferous vegetables are equally impressive. Research has shown that men who eat the most cruciferous vegetables had a 70 percent lower risk of colon cancer than those who ate the least.

To be most effective, cruciferous vegetables should be eaten raw, or just lightly cooked. Overcooking may destory the cancer fighting ingedients of these vegetables.

Now that you know about some of the most common cancer fighting vegetables, here the following "anticancer salad" is made up of seven "little known" vegetables, which also have all the right stuff for fighting cancer

The Super Seven-Ingredient Anti-Cancer Salad!

Much like the cruciferous vegetables above, each of these greens contain certain antioxident compounds that can neutralize "free radicals in your blood. Free radicals are a specific kind of oxygen molecule which can interact in a negative way with your body's DNA, resulting in increased chances for growth and development of cancer cells.

You may have to do some extra searching in your supermarket, or a health food store to find some of these incredible greens, but it will be worth the effort in the long run. Let's end the suspense and tell you about these seven miracle foods:

(1) Oak leaf lettuce — this has greater taste than ordinary lettuce, and has a deep colorful pigment. It very much resembles an ordinary oak leaf you would see on any tree, but don't worry, the taste is far better!

(2) Curly endive — This green is gaining in popularity in America and is becoming increasingly easy to find. It has a thin, almost stringy appearance, like more narrow versions of dandelion leaves. This leaf contains insoluble fiber

which can help prevent intestinal cancer.

(3) Arugula — This is sometimes called roquette. It is a member of the mustard family and somewhat resembles a common dandelion leaf. It contains special cancer inhibiting compounds called indole-3-carbinols.

(4) Watercress — Another type of mustard green, it has a pleasantly pungent, spicy taste. The spicy taste comes from a substance called isothiocyanates, which is believed to be an anti-cancer agent.

(5) Lolla Rossa — Something like oak-leaf lettuce, it has a deep brownish, purplish greenish appearance.

(6) Radicchio — This is a bright purple and yellow vegetable that looks like a cross between regular iceberg lettuce and a cabbage leaf. It has long been used in tossed salads in Italy.

(7) Mizuna — Another type of mustard green, this one is from Japan, it has an exotic flavor. It's leaves have lots of narrow, sharp appendages.

More Anticancer Foods

If its red, orange or yellow — eat it!

That is, eat if it's a vegetable of that color. Of course, meat is red, but meat certainly is not an anticancer food. In fact, diets long on meat and short of vegetables are increasingly viewed as being major contributors to a variety of cancers, especially stomach and colon cancer, as well as breast cancer, lung cancer, liver cancer and others.

Foods that contain beta-carotene are generally deep green, orange or yellow in color. You know what they are — carrots, squash, sweet potatoes, apricots, cantaloupes, pumpkins, and so on. These foods help create something called retinoic acid in your body, which may be a natural cancer-fighting drug in your body.

Tomatoes, although high in sodium, also contain lycopene. This is the pigment that gives tomatoes their red color, but it is also a "free radical" scrubber. Those people with low lycopene levels in their bodies have five-times the risk of cancer in the pancreas.

Powerful tastes, and powerful remedies

Once again garlic asserts itself as a plant of major medicinal properties. Garlic has been positively identified by nutrition researchers as an effective cholesterol blocker, and antifungal agent for people with mold or intestinal yeast infections.

But garlic has proven itself to be an even more powerful cancer fighter. Garlic battles cancer by boosting your body's immune system. The oils and extracts of garlic seem to be poisons to cancer cells. Studies also show that people who eat a lot of garlic and onions have far less stomach and intestinal cancer than those who don't.

Eating all you can of garlic, onions and scallions will provide you with exceptional protection against many types of cancer.

Other fruits and vegetables

If you are a dyed-in-the-wool meat and potatoes person, then this is not good news for you. But all the research points to the conclusion that diets high in fruits and vegetables, and low in meat may be the best know protection against most of the most common kinds of cancer.

The National Cancer Institute recommends fiver or more servings of fruits and vegetables every day for increased immunity against cancer.

Go fishing for cancer protection

But fighting cancer is not all fruits and vegetables. As it turns out, one of the best anticancer agents may also be vitamin D. Your body manufactures vitamin D whenever you are out in the sun. But, as you know, too much sun may lead to skin cancer!

An alternative is foods rich in vitamin D. The best sources of vitamin D are salmon, mackeral, sardines and tuna. Dry cereals and milk also contain significant amounts of vitamin D. So a diet of fruits and vegetables supplemented with an occasional fish dinner will have you well on your way to excellent cancer protection.

Cancer — what to avoid

So far, we've been concentrating on what you should do more of, or eat more of to reduce your chances of getting cancer. But there are also risks in your every day environment that may increase your chances of getting cancer. Let's take a look at some of these.

Cigarettes, alcohol, fat , second hand smoke and ... mouthwash?

Do we even need to remind you of the dangers of these things? By now you have probably accepted the fact that cigarettes cause cancer, but the evidence is also conclusive that second-hand smoke is a definite cancer causer. Many non-smokers, for example, who work in smokey environments, such as bars, are showing lung x-rays and examinations equivalent to two-pack-a-day smokers! If your spouse or another family smokes frequently in the same room with you — you might as wll be smoking yourself!

Also, excessive alcohol, or even small amounts of alcohol taken over long periods of time have been strongly linked to cancer. Even common brands of mouthwash, which contain a percentage of alcohol, have been linked to mouth cancer. Avoid a daily drink of alcohol and you'll lower your cancer risk.

Being overweight seems to be a big factor in causing increased incidence of breast cancer, and other types of cancer, especially in women. Maintaining a low-fat diet and a modest weight is so good for so many other areas of your health, and now it has also shown to be an excellent way to avoid cancer. You should strongly consider a weight loss program based on a low-fat diet and regular exercise.

Chlorinated Water?

Chlorine has long been used to make your water supplies free of harmful bacteria, but it also has become a suspect in causing cancer of the bladder colon or rectum. Studies show that chances of developing these types of cancer are pretty remote — but if one of those remote people is you, that's too high a risk. Fortunately, it is easy to obtain non-chlorinated drinking water at a fairly low cost. Most supermarkes have bulk water supplies of distilled, nonchlorinated water. You can also purchase your own purifying machines that will produce all the drinking water you can use. Studies show the best kind of water to drink is that which is purified by a process know as reverse osmosis. Reverse osmosis machines can be purchased to use in your home, and many common bottled waters on the supermarket shelves use the same process. (See "Water" heading in this book).

Water bed ... electric blanket ... powerlines

Could your warm, comfortable heated water bed or electric blanket give you cancer. It's possible. Covering yourself with an electric blanket exposes your body to current of electromagnetic radiation (EM) that may interfere with your body's normal electronic field. Some researchers suspect that water beds and electric blankets may be the cause of miscarriages, or tumors in some individuals. Check your home and immediate area for other source of EM which you may be exposed to frequently. Some suggestions: nearby powerlines, computers, heating pads, cellular telephones. (Note: See "Powerline Alert!" heading)

Talcum Powder

The two main uses for talcum powder are feminine hygiene and powdering baby's bottoms. Talcum powder used to contain traces of asbestos, but this was eliminated when asbestos became a known cancer agent. But even with asbestos now eliminated from talcum, new evidence suggests that talcum may still be a source of malignancy, especially for women who use it as a feminine hygiene product. Women who use talcum powder on a regular basis have shown as much as three times the vaginal cancer rate as non-users. Many doctors now urge people not to dust babies with talcum powder because there is still no guarantee that it is pure, even of asbestos.

Yes avoid cancer agents ... but please remember this...

Of course, there are many other potential cancer agents in our daily lives, but the danger of talking about every food or substance that may have even the most minute chance of causing cancer leads people to throw up their hand and say: "Hell! Everything causes cancer! You might as well stop living your life in fear of every little thing — just live!"

There's a lot of truth in that statement. But there are also a lot of clear dangers that can be easily avoided, such as smoking, drinking and eating a high fat, high meat diet.

And while avoiding may be difficult, persuing certain other things is easy. Eating more of the cancer fighting foods and vitamins we have listed for you will go a long way in keeping you healthy and free of one of our most deadly and painful killers.

Cholesterol

Time to get to work on your cholesterol problem. Let's take your cholesterol level down percentage by percentage until you find yourself under that magic number of 200 — the level of cholesterol that will rid or ease dozens of health problems — from the dangers of heart disease and cancer to enlarged prostate and diabetes.

Knock Off a Quick 15 Percent — Eat Garlic

If you had to do just one easy thing a day to reduce your cholesterol level by 10 to 15 percent, you would do it, right? Right. Well, all you have to do is swallow a of couple of capsules of powdered garlic every day and you've done it. You can also use whole garlic cloves; just crush them and swallow them with water.

It's as easy as that. Tests are conclusive that simply eating garlic every day will clean your blood of cholesterol by some 10 percent on average — and may help as much as 25 or 30 percent in some people who respond well to garlic therapy.

More and more, garlic is being recognized as a "wonder

food" that not only cleanse your body of harmful fatty acids, but also boosts your immune system to help you fight off diseases from cancer to colds.

Let's Go for More — Vitamins C, E and B-3

Now that you are taking garlic every day, make sure you take tablets of vitamin C, E and B-3 (niacin) everyday. All three of these supplements have shown positive results in lowering cholesterol. Don't overdo these supplements, especially E and niacin. Too much of these two can lead to toxic side effects. But remembering to take one vitamin E and niacin tablet a day will bolster your attack against cholesterol.

Another 5 to 25 Percent — Calcium

Yes, calcium has been pin-pointed as an excellent remedy for high blood pressure, but now it also has been shown to reduce cholesterol levels by 5 percent in the short run, and by as much as 25 percent in the long run — if calcium supplements are taken faithfully over a period of one year or more.

Chromium

Research has shown that taking chromium supplements helps to normalize serum cholesterol increasing the "good" cholesterol while reducing the "bad."

And here's better news: chromium is naturally present in wine and some brands of beer. Be careful though. One glass of wine a day maybe beneficial, but the harmful effects of alcohol multiply quickly with increased dosage.

Super Foods That Fight Cholesterol

Now that you know what supplements you can take to

easily lower your cholesterol level, eating more of these foods will help further.

Fish — Fish oils, especially omega-3, makes blood less prone to clotting. Eskimos rarely suffer heart attacks and their fish-rich diets are probably the reason. Eating the fish itself is far better than taking fish oil supplements. For one thing, you get more fish oil in a single serving of fish than you do in a capsule supplement. Also, fish oil capsules have been linked to some problems, such as bloating, belching, possible diarrhea and other problems.

The best kinds of fish? Mackerel, anchovies, salmon, herring, tuna and others ... but the ones listed here are the easiest to find and contain the most omega-3.

Corn Bran — Eating a spoonful or more of corn bran every day may lower your cholesterol level by as much as 20 percent in time. You can mix corn bran into breads, or swallow it with water or tomato juice.

Carrots — Eat carrots every day and you could trim 15 to 20 percent off your cholesterol level. How hard can it be to eat a couple of carrots per day?

Oat Bran — The public and media went virtually wild a couple of years ago over the potential of oat bran to lower blood cholesterol, but alas, much of it seemed to be unfounded. Still, test in some people seem to point at least circumstantially that oat bran is a good cholesterol fighter. Give it a try. You have nothing to lose and you'll gain some valuable fiber in your diet.

What To Do With the Rest of Your Diet

Now that we have told you about all the supplements and foods that you can easily take to lower your cholesterol level, lets talk about the rest of your general diet, and let's start with the good news — you don't even have to give up red meat!

Red Meats — Yes, you can still include red meat in your diet as long as you choose lean cuts and make sure that you trim the fat. Also, don't make meat the primary portion of your diet.

Fruits and Vegetables — Do we even have to tell you this? Increasing the amount of fruits and vegetables in your diet will dramatically reduce the level of cholesterol in your body. That's a hard scientific fact. Do it!

Milk — Come on! Choose 2 percent or skim milk — get used to it! If you do, you will eliminate a major source of cholesterol in your daily life.

Use Margarine — Its not much better than butter, but certain brands are becoming so low fat free and cholesterol free that it only makes sense to choose them over butter.

Jettison the Coffee — You wouldn't normally associate coffee with a higher cholesterol level, especially since coffee has been shown to be an effective appetite suppresant and weight loss agent. But it's only the caffeine in coffee that lowers your appetite. Coffee contains dozens of other oils and by-products that have been linked to higher cholesterol levels. No more than two cups a day will eliminate this possible source of higher cholesterol in your blood.

What To Do With Your Lifestyle

Of course, exercise has been shown to be a very effective anti-cholesterol activity. It increases your body's ability to clear away fat build-up in your blood after meals. Studies have shown that runners clear fat from their bodies 70 percent faster than non-runners. It even works while they are not running because regular exercise changes the biochemical activity of your body in a way that helps it deal with unwanted fats and balance the other nutrients of your body in a more holistic way.

You're on Your Way

If you just try a few or all of the above cholesterol fighting techniques, you'll soon be on your way to a heart healthier life, as well as a much longer, disease-free life.

Three Terrible "C's" — Coffee, Chocolate, Caffeine (Are they the cause of lumps in your breast?)

You probably already know that too much coffee and chocolate are probably not good for you. Both coffee and chocolate contain caffeine and a few other choice oils and acids that are not exactly what the doctor ordered. On the other hand, no one ever died from a little coffee and a candy bar — right? Used in moderation how bad can they be?

Well, coffee, chocolate and caffeine may be a lot more powerful — and a lot worse — to your general state of health than you previously imagined. They may even be a major cause of certain lumps in the breasts of females.

But before we get into that, let's start with the fact that coffee and chocolate are, in fact, powerful, addictive drugs.

A History of Addiction

It would be hard for us in America, or almost anywhere, to imagine life without coffee and chocolate. But these substances, both derivatives of the cocoa bean, were relatively unknown to American and European civilization at one time.

Coffee, tea and cocoa were introduced simultaneously in England in 1650, although coffee from Africa and Arabic lands had been brewed in Europe as early as the year 1100 AD. Coffee was recognized immediately as a powerful stimulant, and was used as much for medicine — as a drug — as it was for drinking.

The Europeans quickly recognized the dangers of too much coffee — addiction, stomach ulcers, stomach cancer, heart conditions, insomnia, tremors and even convulsions in some people.

Coffee was once outlawed as a dangerous drug in Europe, and only those who disobeyed the law and drank coffee in private circles kept it around long enough for laws against it to be repealed in the 1700s.

Soon after that, coffee drinking spread rapidly and addiction to caffeine became "normalized." An addiction that everyone possesses is no longer viewed as an addiction, but the norm.

The same is true of chocolate. Chocolate contains caffeine, but also another stimulant called theobromine. Chocolate's combination of caffeine, theobromine and sugar make it extremely addictive. When chocolate was brought by the Spanish Conquistadors to Europe in the 1500s and early 1600s, it took less than a couple of decades before tons of it were being produced and consumed throughout the continent.

The Dangers

Coffee in moderate amounts — two to three cups per day — is okay for most people, even somewhat beneficial. But like any addictive drug, it's always extremely difficult to stop at a certain limit. Before you know it, you're an eight- 10-20-cup per day drinker.

Drinking coffee in these amounts may cause:

heart problems
diarrhea
Stomach ulcers
mental anxiety
Menstrual problems
incontinence
insomnia
heartburn
dehydration

fatigue
Nervousness
Convulsions
hypertension
hot flashes
headaches
panic attacks
hiatal hernia

In addition to bringing on some of these diseases, coffee can also make some of your existing conditions a lot worse, especially people who have arthritis, or similar inflammatory diseases.

Lumps in the breast from coffee?

Medical research has linked coffee, tea, chocolate and caffeine to fibrocystic breast disease (FBD), or breast lumps. FBD lumps are noncancerous, but may present a hazard to your health nevertheless.

In some studies, women who completely eliminated coffee and all other caffeine bearing foods from their diet found that their breast lumps disappeared within 6 months. Of course the studies are not conclusive, but those with FBD have absolutely nothing to lose by giving up caffeine to see if it will get rid of breast lumps.

How to Kick the Three C's

However you give up coffee and chocolate, it's best not to go cold turkey. There's a good chance that you will experience major headaches after giving up coffee because the blood vessels in your brain will expand until they adjust to the absence of caffeine. Treating your headache with over-the-counter drugs may be counterproductive because many contain caffeine themselves! Read the ingredient label before you choose a headache remedy.

Go down gradually by mixing your regular coffee with decaf, perhaps a 50-50 mixture to begin. Work your way to total decaf — and then give up that, too. Even decaffeinated coffee contains a small amount of caffeine, but it also contains a lot of acids, oils and other by products that generally do your body no good.

Everything from yellowed teeth to an aggravated stomach still result from decaf — so give it the boot.
Don't forget all the other foods which contain caffeine as well, including soft drinks, candy, diet pills, some aspirin formulas and others.

What giving up this powerful drug in our lives really gets down to is some will power and substituting other, more benign stimulants. But really, thinking that you need any kind of food or chemical stimulate at all is sort of wrong-headed thinking.

Relying on a food or a drink to pick you up means that you are not trusting the natural energy level of your body. Your alertness and energy will always be adequate if you give your body the balanced foods and liquids it needs, and also the rest and exercise it needs. A 15 minute nap is 10 times better than a cup of coffee and a cigarette, and your long-term energy level will be greatly enhanced as well.

For the sake of your health, give up the "Terrible Three C's" and we guarantee — the overall changes in life will be dramatic.

Colds and Flu

Here's the thing about colds: If you don't treat a cold, it will last a week. If you do treat a cold, it will only last seven days.

The moral of the story is, a cold will usually run its course within a week or so, no matter what cure or remedy you throw at it. The common cold is famous for the fact that is has no cure. But is that still true?

Maybe not. By eating certain foods and doing certain things, you may be able to cut down your cold to a one- or two-day event. On the other hand, there is a lot you can do to make your cold worse and last longer.

First, let's look at some cold fighting strategies:

Feed a cold, Starve a fever?

Is this old bromide true? Yes! according to our best evidence. And it's especially true if you feed your cold the right thing.

So just what should you feed your cold?

Vitamin C

Much has been said and written about the ability of vitamin C to chase away a cold more quickly. The two-time Nobel Prize winning chemist, Linus Pauling, was very big on vitamin C, and he maintained that large doses of the stuff will stop a cold dead in its tracks. Pauling considered vitamin C a "cure" for the common cold.

Well, tons of research has been done on Vitamin C's

relationship to colds. What seems clear is that vitamin C will not prevent a cold, but can help it clear up more quickly.

Researchers at the University of Wisconsin compared cold sufferers who took vitamin C to those who didn't and concluded that 1,000 mg of extra vitamin C per day may shorten a cold by as much as five days. Other, independent studies in Canada and Australia also reached very similar conclusions. So taking a 1,000 mg tablet of vitamin C every day from the time you notice first symptoms will likely put you back in shape much quicker.

Should You Think Zinc?

If you look carefully enough on drug store shelves you will find a certain kind of cold lozenge which contain zinc gluconate. Some very preliminary studies show that zinc may clear up a cold even faster than vitamin C. Try a zinc lozenge if you want, but beware that these medications can cause digestive problems in some people.

Grandma's Chicken Soup

In Scotland, it's called Cock-a-Leekie; in Mexico, Calso de Pollo; in Korea, Paeksuk; in France, Poulet au Pot. Here in America we call it plain old chicken soup. Chicken soup is recognized around the world and by many cultures as an effective remedy for colds, and for good reason.

Studies have shown that chicken soup clears nasal congestion faster than ordinary hot water. Unlike vitamin C or zinc, chicken soup has never been credited with taking days off the duration of a cold, but it provides comfort and nutrition while your symptoms last.

Lots of Liquids?

Drinking a lot during a cold is always recommended and is always good advice. Set yourself a goal of 8 oz. of juice or water every two hours.

Other Cold Pointers

(a) Avoid excessively cold temperatures and tiring yourself out.

(b) Take to your bed, especially if you have a fever.

(c) Gargle with a hot salt solution. Use 1 teaspoon in 8 oz. glass of water, which should be heated to the temperature of hot tea or coffee.

(d) Aspirin or Tylenol is almost always helpful

Keep this in mind

Scientists say the average cold lasts nine days. Anything that lasts longer than two weeks may be something other than a cold, such as an allergy, sinus infection, flu, or something worse. If your symptoms linger, if you have excessive fever, if you develop white or yellow patches on your tonsils or throat, or other similar conditions, see a doctor.

The Flu

If you take all the symptoms of a common cold, make them five times more severe and longer lasting, you pretty much have a description of flu or influenza.

If a cold is a fender bender, the flu is a head-on collision.

And really, the treatment is about the same. Try vitamin C,

zinc, chicken soup and lots of liquids, rest, aspirin, although you shouldn't expect these to be as effective against the flu.

In fact, the flu will probably force you into your bed for atleast a day or two. The fever and aches associated with the flu make your life miserable for a good (or a bad) two weeks.

But unlike the common cold, the flu can be prevented. Flu vaccines are widely available, and it may save you tons of pain and misery to get yourself a needle in the arm, leg — or wherever they put those things these days.

Best time to get a flu shot is October or November.

The Stomach Flu

A more specific kind of flu is one that attacks your stomach and digestive system. Nausea, vomiting, diarrhea are commonly blamed on stomach flu, and some kind of virus is the cause of 90 percent of such cases. Other causes may be food poisoning or certain parasites, such as giardia or endamoeba, which causes amoebic dysentery.

What to do about stomach flu

(a) Rest in bed until all nausea, vomiting, diarrhea and fever are gone. Staying upright increases the amount of fluids lost to diarrhea, which saps your energy.

(b) If vomiting persists, no food and only ice chips to maintain moisture levels for first day. When vomiting stops, go to clear liquids. Probably on day two of your illness. After a day or liquids, try soft foods, such as bananas, oatmeal, mashed or baked potatoes, etc. Start eating solid foods when your stomach feels able to handle it.

(C) Avoid cigarettes, alcohol, most fruits (although bananas may help curb diarrhea) and spicy foods for five days.

(d) Always maintain fluid levels — dehydration is a major danger during stomach flu and can lead to serious complications.

See a doctor if symptoms are severe and show no signs of clearing up after a day or so.

Colon Problems

Colitis

Colitis, or irritable colon, may be the result of several causes, from stomach flu, to ulcers or cancer. Colitis basically is the inflammation of the large bowel, or colon. There are many minor types of colitis, but some are serious and can be deadly.

Stop it from happening

Perhaps the best way to deal with colon problems are to stop them from happening in the first place. Cancer of the colon can be avoided if people have frequent check-ups which include sample of stool. Some 95 percent of all colon cancers can be cured if they are detected early enough, and the only way to do that is with check-ups at least three times per year, especially for people over 50.

Treating your colon to the proper diet will also reduce or even eliminate your chances of developing colon problems. Eating a lot of high fat, hard-to-digest food will keep you blocked up and will lead to the formation of certain pockets in your colon that can develop into ulcers or cancer.

A high-fiber diet long on fruits and vegetable and short on meats, cheeses and breads will keep the contents of your colon moving along. A daily helping of beans, wheat bran, rice, bulgar, oat bran, corn bran and just about any other vegetable product will keep your colon clean and less likely to contract an illness.

And smoking is not only hard on your lungs — it also has many negative effects on digestion, your stomach and colon. Smoking is closely linked to higher rates of colon cancer — so kick the habit!

Ulcerative Colitis

This is a painful inflammation of the colon which can produce blood in your stool, diarrhea and lots of pain. Once you develop ulcerative colitis, drugs and a doctor's help are about the only way you can deal with the problem. Once again, you can do much to prevent your chance of developing ulcerative colitis by maintaining a high fiber diet. Starting a high fiber diet after you contract the disease may also help you recover lots quicker. But if you suspect you have ulcerative colitis, don't fool around, see a doctor.

Crohn's Disease

Very similar to ulcerative colitis, this disease is distinguished from the former by the fact that ulcerative colitis is restricted to the large bowel, although most agree there isn't a dime's worth of difference between the two. Crohn's Disease, sometimes called granulomatous enterocolitis, is a condition in which ulcers appear on the small or large intestines along with granulomas, which are tumor-like masses of an inflammatory nature.

About 10,000 people contract this disease every year. It is marked by cramping, pain, diarrhea, fever and bleeding.

There is no known cause for Crohn's Disease and no known cure. Your doctor will probably prescribe steroids to help you out. One of the best ways to control this painful affliction is with a sensible, high-fiber diet that skips the harmful sweets and caffeines. During times of diarrhea, however, which is a frequent symptom of Crohn's, you may want to limit your fruits and vegetables to help your colon catch up and firm up a bit. In general, though, eat only stomach friendly, easy-to-digest foods to prevent flare-ups, and see a doctor.

Diverticular Disease

Speaking of the colon, a somewhat common disease effecting that part of your body is called diverticulosis, or in its worse stage, diverticulitis. Diverticulosis is when small sacks push out through the outer wall of the large intestine and just sort of hang there. If that doesn't sound painful enough, these sacks can become inflamed and irritated, and then you have a real pain to deal with.

Surprisingly, though, many people can have this condition without knowing it. But in others it can cause tremendous pain. The symptoms of diverticular disease are cramping pains, constipation and possibly diarrhea. If the condition gets worse, the result can be fever, severe pain, internal bleeding, blood in the stools, or even a blocked colon. In that case, you need a doctor and possibly surgery.

But the good news about diverticular disease is that you can start preventing it today with a sensible, high-fiber diet. While it was once believed that diverticular disease was for old folks only, it is now believed that poor diet is the biggest cause.

Studies showed simply that people who eat too much meat and dairy products, and who don't eat enough vegetables and fiber are as much as 100 times more likely to develop diverticulitis at some time in their life.

People who have already developed diverticulitis can ease their condition considerably   by adding bran and other forms of fiber to their diet. Add a greater amount of beans and brown rice to your diet, as well as oat bran or oat flakes. Eating apples and whole grain bread, blueberries and brussels sprouts, lettuce and cucumbers will also give you an excellent fiber boost.

Get into your higher fiber diet slowly. If you are not used to a high-fiber diet, you could develop a lot of gas, bloating, even mild diarrhea. But if you start slow and be consistent about getting more fiber into your diet, you'll have no problem whatsoever.

Whatever you do, don't start taking artificial laxatives on a daily basis to aid your bowel movements. Using artificial laxatives on a regular basis is foolhardy, and may cause you further problems. But a bulking agent, such as Metamucil, can be helpful and serve as a laxative in itself.

Remember that coffee, chocolate and other sources of caffeine can cause considerable colon irritation and inflammation. If you are having stomach cramps and the other symptoms of diverticulitis, coffee and chocolate are not for you.

In general, though, avoid the meats, cheeses and white breads, and increase all fruits and vegetables in your diet. Doing so will help you say good-bye to diverticular disease for good.

Polyps of the Colon

A polyp is usually a noncancerous growth on the wall of your intestine, usually composed of mucus membranes. These can also appear very near your rectum and are sometimes called rectal polyps if they are near the rectal opening. Polyps can also be cancerous and can grow just about anywhere in your body, not just in your colon.

Polyp growth probably has more to do with genetics and old age as it does with other contributing factors. Only a doctor can tell you if you have a polyp on your colon, and only a doctor can determine if it's cancerous or not. Either way, a colon polyp is something that must be dealt with through surgery.

Still, it is always good advice to treat your colon properly over your lifetime. If you smoke, eat a lot of sugar and fat, drink too much alcohol and coffee, then you are doing everything you can to punish your colon. Bad habits have a way of cropping up on you later in life — sometimes in the form of cancerous polyps on your colon.

Take care of your colon with a high-fiber, low-fat diet and don't smoke, and colon polyps may be something you never have to worry about.

Constipation

You don't have to be a genius to know what's causing your constipation — and thus how to fix it — although there may be some hidden causes of constipation you never knew about. But let's look at the common problems first.

It's what you eat (or don't eat)

If you are constipated, you likely are not getting enough fiber in your diet. It's just as simple as that. If you live on meat, potatoes, and bread only, don't be surprised if you get stopped up now and then.

The solution is as simple as eating more fruits and vegetables (beyond potatoes) including the many well known colon movers — stewed prunes, prune juice, bananas, beans, rice, wheat bran, bulgar, and so on. Just about any fruit or vegetable will do wonders for your regularity.

Too many commercially prepared foods, such as frozen dinners and restaurant food, will contribute to your constipation because they simply don't have a proper proportion of fiber within them.

What about laxatives?

What about forgetting them? You might as well because research shows that laxatives do very little to ease constipation. They can also be harmful, especially to elderly people. Studies show that too frequent use of laxatives depletes calcium in the body which can lead to bone thinning and osteoporosis.

Prescription drugs can be more potent, but you need a doctor to get those. And why would you spend money on a doctor when all you have to do is eat a little more fruit and vegetables every day?

Hidden causes of constipation

Even if you are getting enough bulk in your diet, you may be taking a prescription drug that is inhibiting your bowel movements. Some blood pressure drugs and many pain killers, such as Percodan and Codeine, have been known to cause constipation. If you suspect your prescription drugs are your problem, ask the doctor you got them from.

Beware of a more serious problem

Sometimes constipation can be the result of some other

serious illness. If you have chronic or persistent constipation, even if your diet is high in fiber, you'd better see a doctor.

Corns

Are you crowding your toes? Then you are lookin' for corns. Corns on your feet, that is. Yes, wearing your shoes too tight will give you corns. Also, friction between your foot and the shoe will cause corns.

We don't care how fashionable or good those shoes look — if they're causing corns, why not get rid of them? If you are already getting corns, your shoes may be doing more serious, long-term damage to your feet. If you are crowding your toes, you may be forcing the bones in your feet to take a shape they weren't designed for. If your foot is still growing, you may end up with a deformed foot which will require surgery in later years.

A more roomy shoe combined with some padding over your corns is about all you can do to ease up the pain during the day when you need to wear shoes. (Can you get by in your job without shoes? Maybe you can!) If you have a desk job, give your feet all the relief you can by slipping off your shoes under your desk for as long as you can. The more chance you give your corns to heal the better.

There's always soaking

Of course, your good common sense tells you that soaking will help your corns — and it will. In fact, soaking your feet every night in warm water with a bit of vinegar will do much more than the over-the-counter drugs you can buy for corn removal.

None of the above?

If new shoes, soaking and over-the-counter drugs don't work, and sometimes they don't, having your corns surgically removed can be incredibly quick and easy. You may not even need a doctor to do it. A qualified nurse or a physician's assistant can perform the procedure, usually in less than 15 minutes! It'll cost you a few bucks, but your problem will be gone for good! (Unless you choose that new pair of shoes you've had your eye on, and you know what we mean).

Colors: Their Amazing Power to Heal

Do you think it's possible to cure a nasty, lingering cold by shining a blue light on yourself, or by applying a blue-colored oil to your throat and chest? Or might it be possible to lower your blood pressure by exposing yourself to black, blue and green colors?

As outlandish as this might seem, many people are finding that something as simple as color has tremendous potential to heal sickness, and maintain good health.

If you stop a minute to give it some thought, the fact that color can affect our bodies, minds and emotions is not such a strange concept. After all, have you ever felt "red with rage?" What do you feel like when you're "in the pink?" How about "feeling blue" or "green with jealousy?" Have you ever been through a "black depression?"

It seems that we have subconsciously been associating colors with our physical and mental health for quite some time. Colors have unconsciously worked their way into our description of how we feel — perhaps they can do more to improve or even heal our minds and bodies.

For example, it's easy to associate the color red with anger, stress and pressure. With these emotions come physiological changes in the body, including high blood pressure, decreased immunity to disease, stress on the heart, strokes, and others.

Researchers in Great Britain have been experimenting with color therapies to treat a variety of illnesses, including high blood pressure and related conditions.

People who have a history of high blood pressure and job stress were instructed in a mental visualization technique in which each person was taught to imagine themselves surrounded by a sphere of cool, blue light. They were also told to visualize the light penetrating their bodies and flooding every cell and bone with its cooling energy. In addition, the patients were routinely exposed to various shades of blue lamp light, and were given massages with blue-tinted oils.

The results were dramatic. Most patients had a marked decrease in their blood pressure, and all of them reported feeling less stressed mentally, and better able to cope with the stress of their jobs or daily lives.

Of course, lower blood pressure means a healthier heart, fewer migraine headaches and a variety of other healthful benefits — all resulting from the mere application of blue light.

Other people have healed common cold and sore throats by applying blue-colored oils to their throats and chests.

Light therapy has made its way into our everyday culture in many other ways.

Prison officials, for example, have long known that "bubble gum pink is an excellent color for the walls of jail cells. The color pink seems to have a calming, soothing effect on people, making them less likely to respond aggressively, or feel anger. Studies of prisons that switched their walls from gray or green colors to pink showed a marked improvement in prisoner behavior. Even prisoners who were color blind responded favorably to pink walls and fluorescent pink lights!

We all know that "being in the pink" is associated with a calm, relaxed, pleasant feeling.

Other researches have shown that a turquoise light had a healing effect on arthritis, and that green, orange, red and bright sunshine yellow were helpful in bringing people out of depression.

Yellow and gold lights have shown to be beneficial to liver, kidney, spleen, stomach/digestions, and nervous system.

How You Can Use Colors For Your Better Health

Color therapy has its origins in the lost, ancient healing arts of the distant past.

The ancient Greeks and Egyptions considered the sun to be the source of all healing, and they established color-healing temples in Thebes and Heliopolis.

After being lost and forgotten for centuries, light therapy made a comeback in the late 1800's. In a book published in 1976, called Blue and Sun-Lights, researcher Augustus Pleasanton found that light from the sun and artificial sources, when focused properly, were able to stimulate the nervous system, various glands and secretory organs of animals and people. Sunlight filtered through a blue or red glass relaxed or accelerated the human nervous system.

According to these sources and others, there is much you can do via color therapy to improve your general level of health. Here is a color-balancing exercise you can try once per day, and then judge the results for yourself:

The Seven Colors of the Body

Both ancient and modern practitioners agree that certain parts or areas of the body are associated with specific energy centers, also called "chakras," each of which are associated with a particular color. The colors are those of the rainbow: red, orange, yellow, green, blue, indigo and violet. You can remember these colors in the proper order by thinking of the name "Roy G. Biv." Each letter in the name is the first of the color it represents.

To ensure your colored energy centers are in harmony, each chakra should be fully opened and balanced. You can do that be visualizing each energy center as glowing with its proper color. This will set in motion the regenerative and healing process within the body.

The colors correspond to the body as follows:

(1) The energy center at the base of your spine is red.

(2) The area of your reproductive organs is orange.

(3) The area of your stomach or naval is yellow.

(4) The area centred on your heart is green.

(5) Your throat area is blue.

(6) A point on your forehead above and slightly between your eyes is indigo.

(7) The crown of your head is violet.

To balance and align these color centers, find a quite place where you can be undisturbed by people or telephones for aboutt 20 minutes.

Lay flat on your back with hands at your sides. Take three deep, slow breaths to relax yourself and put yourself into a quiet state of mind.

Once you have taken a minute or two to breathe and clear your head, begin to visualize a small orb of violet light at the top of your head. You can make it any size that seems right to you — the size of a gold ball, apple, or whatever comes to you as appropriate.

Try to hold the image in your mind of a violet orb at the top of your head for a minute or two, going through several slow in and out breaths.

Once you have the violet orb at the top of your head clearly in place, go to the next energy center in the middle of your forehead. Again, visualize an indigo orb there in your forehead, and let it be there for a minute of two.

Now do the same thing for the rest of the energy centers: blue for the throat, green for the heart, yellow for the stomach, orange for the sexual organs and, finally, red for the base of the spine.

After about 15 minutes, you should have visualized and energized the color centre of your body. Next you may want to envision a narrow band of light connecting the seven glowing orbs in a straight line from the top of your head down through your spine and all the way to your feet.

After you've completed the exercise, just let go and relax for a few minutes. The whole process can last about 20 minutes, more or less, or as long as you would like it to.

Balancing your color centers this way combines a kind of calming meditation with the exciting new possibilities of color therapy. After taking time to perform this color-balancing process for two or three weeks in a row, it would be amazing if you would not notice the energizing and lifting effect this can have on your overall health. Especially for those who suffer from stress, high blood pressure, migraine headaches, poor digestion and heart problems, this exercise may change your entire life, and could eliminate these problems for good.

For more intensive color therapy ideas, or to find out more about this fascinating area of holistic health, pick books called , "What Color Are You?" by Annie Wilson and Lilla Bek; "The Seven Keys to Color Healing", by Roland Hunt; "Colour Therapy ",by Mary Anderson.

Dandruff

Television commercials have come to make us all believe that dandruff is an unimaginably hideous problem on par with global thermonuclear war, famine, invasion of the earth by loathsome squid men from outer space — and worse.

Having dandruff in your hair and on your shoulders instantly identifies you as a loser, an unclean person, a nightmare date and an unwanted sexual partner.

Is dandruff as bad as all that?

Well, anything we can tell you is unlikely to counteract the years of media conditioning which has made us all fear and despise dandruff more than coming of the AntiChrist himself. But keep it in perspective. In short, you'll live.

Although far from a life-threatening medical condition, dandruff is still an unwanted skin condition that, if left untreated, can get worse or develop into something even more unsightly, such as ugly yellow scaling and patches encrusted on your scalp.

Contrary to what you might think, dandruff is not caused by dry skin, but by oily skin. So don't try to treat your dandruff with lotions and skin creams that contain oil. That'll probably make the problem worse.

The Shampoos

You've seen all the over-the-counter products. Do they work? By and large—yes! So why not use them? Fighting dandruff has become a complex over-the-counter science and the lucrative market these products represent makes an ever-more-effective supply available to us. Take advantage of them! You'll soon find out for yourselves whether they work or not. Be cognizant of the fact that each brand has its own formula, or specific concentration of a specific active ingredient. Get familiar with them. You will soon learn which ones suit you best.

Be sure you give your anti-dandruff shampoo enough time to work. Let it stay on your scalp for at least five minutes or longer if you can. A good way to use dandruff shampoos is during a long bath. Lather up your head first, then sit back and enjoy yourself for as long as you want. Rinse when you're ready to exit the tub. This will give the active ingredient in the shampoo to work its magic.

What if the shampoos don't work?

If they don't, you may have a problem that is something worse than plain dandruff. You may have dermatitis, tho beginnings of psoriasis, eczema or some other skin condition. These manifest themselves with much heavier dandruff, scales and crusting, red patches and more. If you suspect that is so, see the sections in this book under those specific conditions to see what you can do to ease or eliminate them.

A bit of Sunshine

Most people notice that their dandruff is less severe in the summer and it's probably due to some sunshine. As we said, dandruff is the result of oily skin, not dry skin, so the sun's drying effect probably does the trick. Of course, too much sun will dry out and damage your skin, and may result in another form of dandruff associated with skin that is too dry.

Try some zinc

Zinc is a vitamin closely associated with healthy skin. If you have a zinc deficiency, it may contribute to your dandruff. Try a zinc supplement for a couple of months, but don't overdo it. Too much zinc will have toxic side-effects on your body. One zinc tablet a day, and no more, will be all you need.

Dental Problems

We've come a long way in the dental sciences. These days, many people age 25 and under have never had a single cavity in their entire lives!

For those of you who are 30 or over, that seems amazing beyond belief. But just 20 or 30 years ago, prevention was not as much on the agenda as it is today. It wasn't uncommon for a child in the 1960s to have a dentist find a half-dozen cavities, or teeth that needed at least some kind of work.

The reason ordinary tooth decay is on the decline is an emphasis on brushing, flossing — and fluoride in our water supply. In fact, fluoride did for tooth decay what penecillin did for infections.

There's a lesson in all this: you are never too old to start a good preventative dental health program. Starting today, brush after every meal, floss every night before you go to bed, and get a regular check-up — say every six months — and your dental problems will soon be nonexistent.

Cheddar cheese it

You may also want to eat an occasional sliver of cheddar cheese, or just about any hard cheese. The enzymes and other chemicals found in cheese kill the kind of bacteria most likely to cause tooth decay and balances the acidity in your mouth. Of course, cheese is a high fat, high cholesterol food and not good for you in large quantities. But a slice or so once a day won't hurt, and it will help your teeth.

What about tooth pain?

So what if you have a toothache right now? Here are some easy, emergency pain-killing things you can do for a toothache:

Cloves for pain

Until you can get to a dentist to get to the "root" of the problem, try applying oil of cloves to your painful tooth. This is an oil extracted from whole cloves, a kitchen spice commonly used to flavor apple cider and pumpkin pie. The oil in these cloves can numb the nerves in your tooth that are signalling your brain that something is wrong with this tooth.

Oil of cloves contains a chemical called eugenol, which is a topical anesthetic.

You can buy oil of cloves in many grocery stores and in most health food stores. Simply rub the oil on with your finger or a cotton swab.

If you don't have any oil of cloves handy, you may have whole cloves in your spice drawer. Place a couple of them next to your tooth after you have soaked them in hot water for a few minutes to activate the oils.

Aspirins

Aspirins work incredibly well on tooth ache pain, especially aspirin formulas that also contain caffeine. Pop a couple if you can't get to the dentist for awhile ... but eat them! ... don't place them directly on your gum. That may cause your gum to bleed and will lead to an even bigger ache.

Avoid Sugar

Sugar in an open cavity is like pouring salt in an open wound. Sugar in your cavity sets up a process of osmosis within the liquids of your cavity walls, causing the tissue around the tooth to pull and constrict. The result is more pain.

Warm or cold

Sometimes just warming up your tooth will ease the pain. Swirling your mouth with warm water will gently warm up the tooth. Just the opposite — ice — may help if you don't have dental sensitivity to cold.

Salt water

Salt water has long been known to have a numbing affect on teeth and gums. Mix a teaspoon of salt with an 8 oz. glass of warm water and swirl that around in your mouth.

Gum Disease

If your gums start to bleed and you have bad breath; if your teeth hurt and some are even starting to become loose, you probably have gum disease. If your teeth are already starting to wiggle in their sockets you may have periodontitis or pyorrhea.

An early, less serious form of periodontitis is the more well known gum disease called gingivitis. Many mouth washes stake much of their sales power on the fact that they can prevent gingivitis, but the claims are almost certainly overblown. If you rely on mouthwash alone to keep your teeth and gums free of disease, you'll soon be grinning with a snaggle-toothed face.

If you already have gum disease

If you already have gum disease, you are in serious need of a thorough cleaning of your teeth and gums by a qualified professional. If you try to brush, floss and mouthwash your way back to healthy gums, you will probably fail because you need to remove many tiny pockets of plaque and tartar that have become lodged throughout your teeth.

Prevention is the way to go

If you have mild gum disease, a good brushing and flossing may clear up your problem. You can also try a rinse made up of one-third hydrogen peroxide and two-thirds water. Just make sure you get your teeth as clean as possible and get in all the nooks and crannies!

Frequent flushing will help

Using a dental water irrigation device can be very effective in removing harmful bacteria from hidden pockets in your gums that brushes and floss can't get to.

Get more vitamin C

Low levels of vitamin C have been linked to bleeding of the gums in a number of diseases. People with scurvy, for example, which is a vitamin C deficiency disease, are characterized by profusely bleeding gums. To help you gums heal faster and to be generally more healthy, take vitamin C supplements and eat lots of foods high in vitamin C.

Depression

The "Big D". That's what we should call depression because it's such a big problem for so very many people. Depression hits 100 percent of all people at least some of the time. Millions of people are depressed a lot, or all the time.

Depression is sometimes called "the common cold" of mental illness. Everyone gets it now and then. Like a cold, it can come and go, or become entrenched and lead to something worse.

Curiously, many people who are depressed have a lot of doubts about their condition. Are you really depressed, or are you just feeling bad? What's the difference between mild depression and major depression? Maybe it's just loneliness? Do you need a psychiatrist to tell you if you're "really" depressed? Is depression just self pity, or are there good reasons to be depressed? Does depression get worse and worse if it goes untreated, or can it go away by itself?

These and others are all difficult questions to answer. One way of trying to understand depression is to look at what psychology has to say about it. But if you do that, you could spend years in the library or sitting through university classes studying depression, which science has turned into a complex and far reaching problem.

Also, the definitions supplied to us by psychology are heavily semantic — that is — they depend a lot on the listing of clinical terms and descriptions, such as: dejected mood, self loathing, internal negativity, pessimistic, fatigue, feelings of worthlessness, sad faced, distorted self image, low self-esteem and on and on.

Most people find, however, that giving their specific depression a name doesn't do much to get rid of it.

Isn't it just life?

A lot of people have come to the conclusion that depression is the only "normal" way to feel in today's difficult world. With all the crime, war, diseases, financial difficulty, overpopulation, pollution and other stuff to worry about, who in their right mind is not depressed?!

There's probably some truth to that, but, at best, that's an empty observation and, at worst, a non-solution. Saying that depression is "just life" does nothing to make us feel better, and that's what we want — we want to feel joy, peace, satisfation, fulfillment, laughter and so on.

So how about a common sense approach?

For our purposes, let's just keep it simple. If you feel bad — that's it then — you just feel bad. Don't go out and pay a psychologist $50 per hour for six months to reach the same conclusion. Just acknowledge it without trying to draw any deep meaning from it. You know how you feel. You may not know why — but maybe it's not that important if you haven't pin-pointed the exact cause just yet.

Of course, there may be some very obvious reasons why you are depressed. Perhaps someone you love has died or is seriously ill. Maybe you have terrible financial difficulties. Maybe you are physically ill. Maybe your pet has died. Maybe you think the world is going to hell in a hand-basket.

Whatever the reason, you should ask yourself very frankly if you are willing to get rid of your depression. What are you going to do about it right now? Obviously, you can't bring back someone who has died, but you can find a way to cope with it and bring yourself back from your depression. Obviously, you can't fix your financial difficulties overnight, but you can take one small step today that will move you towards solving the problem.

Try the HALT formula

HALT stands for "hungry, angry, lonely, tired."

If you are feeling bad, there is a strong chance that one of the above is causing it. Let's look at them one at a time:

(1) Hungry — Improper nutrition can cause depression in many ways. If you don't get enough to eat, whether it's from poverty or just the fact that you forget to eat when you should, the result can be depression. Eating the wrong kinds of food can also bring you down. If you live on junk food and sweets, you are flirting with depression. Your brain needs a well-balanced diet to keep you happy and healthy, so if you treat your body like a dumpground for Twinkies, depression may be a warning sign that you need to clean up your act.

More specifically, studies have linked low levels of vitamin B-6 to depression and obsessive-compulsive disorders. Vitamin B-6 is needed for your body to make a brain chemical called serotonin. Serotonin may be a major factor in depression, so getting enough of it and vitamin B-6 may really help you out.

Here are some foods that are high in vitamin B-6:

Brown rice	wheat germ
whole wheat	oats
rye	cabbage
beets	oranges
lemons	bananas
avocados	cantaloupe
walnuts	filberts
carrots	sunflower seeds

And many others. Increase your intake of all of the above, however, and they will help you fight off glum moods.

Don't eat ...

Sweets are one of the worst things you can give to your sullen nature. Soothing your feelings with a chocolate sundae or a box of chocolates can really bring you down. When you eat refined sugar, your body reacts by pumping insulin into your bloodstream, and insulin can be a major mood downer.

In general, paying attention to the "H" in the HALT formula is an important weapon against depression. Do yourself a favor and improve your diet.

(2) Angry — Are you really ticked off at someone, at something about your life, or maybe even at yourself? Unresolved anger, which has been pushed down and forgotten may be festering inside you somewhere, sapping your energy and causing depression. The way to deal with anger is to confront it and discharge it. And the only way to do that is to cut loose — but you must find a safe way to do it! If you are really ticked off at your husband, don't bash him in the head with a baseball bat! Bash a watermelon instead and pretend it's your husband. Or try punching a pillow or performing some sort of strenuous exercise. The point is, you need to blow off steam in a way that does not hurt yourself or others. Screaming at the top of your lungs when your are alone can really get a lot off your chest. Having a good cry (as long as it does not become self-pity) can help you get it all out. Whatever method you choose, after you discharge your anger, your emotional self will be relieved of a heavy burden and you will be free to climb the ladder of happiness.

(3) Lonely — Some psychologists say that loneliness is the number one cause of emotional probelms in our country. Today, millions of people are lonely. Why? Well, any thorough discussion of that would lead us into a lot of complex areas, like the break down of the nuclear family, and so on, but let's stay grounded in our simple common sense approach.

Depression and loneliness go hand-in-hand. Human beings are social animals by nature. Some people like to be alone, but most of us need the comfort and support of family, friends and even pets. In fact, recent studies by Swedish researchers suggest that loneliness not only leads to depression, but also may take years off your life. Studies of Swedish men showed that early death rates are significantly higher among men who live alone, and who reported that they had no one to share troubling times with.

If you are depressed right now, take a look at your life and see if you have someone or some people that you can turn to when you are feeling down. If your are estranged from your family, a spouse or your children, maybe it's time to take the first step to patch things up. If you don't have a family, go out and make a new friend. You could also join a club or take up a sport that will introduce yourself to new people.

Whatever you decide to do, getting rid of loneliness may be the very thing you need to do to beat your depression.

(4) Tired — Are you getting enough sleep? Being tired and run down is closely linked to a depressed mental state. An old saying goes something like this: "There's nothing in the world that a hot bath and a good night's sleep can't cure." Well, a good night's sleep may not heal two broken legs, but it can blow away your depression.

In our high stress lives, many of us lose track of just how much we sleep. It's safe to say that anyone who is depressed, and who is getting less than eight hours sleep per night, may be experiencing depression brought on by sleep deprivation. Simply paying more attention to how many hours of shut-eye you get every day may make all the difference in the world. It will give your body chemistry the chance it needs to re-balance itself. It will clear your mind and give you a fresh perspective.

And be aware: every person is unique and has sleep requirements that are individual to that person. Did you know that Albert Einstein slept 10 hours a night? If he got anything less, he felt dizzy, disoriented and unable to think during the day. On the other hand, another genius, Thomas Edison, never slept more than three or four hours per night.

When it comes to sleep, are you an Einstein or an Edison?

Find out. Try adjusting the number of hours you sleep until you feel comfortable with it. If you need 10 hours — then that's what you should get. If you don't think it's macho, or if you think sleeping 10 hours per night is being lazy you're sadly mistaken. Getting the proper amount of sleep your body requires is good, healthy common sense. It's true you will have fewer waking hours, but you'll burn brighter during those hours, you'll get more done, you'll make fewer mistakes — and you'll be happier.

So remember ...

If you're depressed, go through the HALT formula. It may be one of the factors, or all four of them that are making you blue. Deal with them, and you'll soon be in the pink.

SOME OTHER DEPRESSION POINTERS

Wean yourself from television

Ever heard that statement? "Garbage in, garbage out." Even if you are lonely, turning to your television for comfort and companionship can be the worst thing you can do. First of all, it will isolate you even more because you'll be less likely to go out and make new friends. You'll soon be more lonely and miserable than ever.

Second, studies show that television not only slows down the mind, it also slows down your body chemistry. Watching too much television sets you up mentally and physically to be depressed. TV is full of violent images and also images of fantasies and riches that are unrealistic, and which can never be achieved by the average person. TV makes you feel like a loser because real life can never match up to the unreal world of the small screen.

Quitting television can be as difficult as quitting smoking so try to wean yourself gradually, or just quit cold turkey, but make the effort.

Check out SAD

Many people find that they feel great in the summer, but miserable in the winter. The problem may be SAD, or Seasonal Affective Disorder. This is a condition which results from reduced levels of sunlight. SAD is associated with the pineal gland, which is sometimes called "The Third Eye" in esoteric circles. The pineal gland is located directly between your eyes on your forehead. When the amount of sunlight striking the pineal gland is reduced, it produces less of certain brain chemcials which help maintain your mood.

Fixing SAD can be a simple as getting more sunlight. How do you do that during the dark days of winter? Well, just about any health care supply store, and some health food stores, stock lamps which produce the same kind of light radiation that the sun produces. Sitting in front of this light for an extra hour in the morning before the sun comes up, or after it goes down, can mimic the effect of a longer, summer day. Your pineal gland will begin kicking out the brain chemicals you need to take you from SAD to GLAD.

Avoid depressants

Many drugs and foods are depressants. The big one, of course, is alcohol. A lot of people say they are "feeling good" when they have a couple of drinks. But ultimately, alcohol teaches your body chemistry the lesson of depression. Avoid alcohol and you'll keep a major mood suppressor off your back.

As we mentioned earlier, sweets, especially chocolate have chemicals within them associated with depression. Also, drinking too much coffee can cause depression because it causes you to urinate more. When you urinate more, you deplete your body of depression-fighting substances, such as potassium and vitamin B-6. So kick the coffee, eat a banana and cheer up!

Diabetes

Because diabetes is a disease so closely associated with the nutritional needs and functions of the body, people who are diabetic would be remiss if they did not take a hard look at what they eat, and take advantage of the tremendous amount of knowledge that is available about controlling diabetes with diet.

Before you attempt home remedies to fight your disease, make sure you know what kind of diabetes you have — Type I or Type II. Type I is usually a children's disease and results from a lack of the natural body hormone called insulin. It's also sometimes called "insulin dependent diabetes." People with Type I need insulin injections. Type II diabetes is the result of having too much of the insulin your body produces naturally, and most often occurs in adults.

Fortunately, 90 percent of all diabetics — about 9 million people — are of Type II diabetes, which can be more easily treated with diet and avoidance of harmful foods.

One of the very best way to battle Type II diabetes is with a high-carbohydrate, high-fiber diet. In a study conducted by Dr. James Anderson of the University of Kentucky School of Medicine, 13 people put on such a diet produced these results:

• Blood sugar dropped from 179 for people on a standard diet to just 119.

• After just a few weeks on the diet, five of the men were able to quit their diabetes medication.

• Five other men were able to reduce or eliminate their insulin injections

• Blood cholesterol levels improved and blood triglycerides dropped 15 percent.

So here are the food-types recommended by the American Diabetes Association.

Carbohydrates: 50-60 percent

Protein: 12-20 percent

Fats: No more than 30 percent

Don't forget fiber

Fiber has been shown to be tremendously beneficial to diabetics. Eat a lot of whole wheat products, barley, oats, beans of all sorts, vegetables and fruits to obtain maximum fiber in your diet.

Avoid Alcohol at All Costs

Alcohol can have the very same effect on a diabetic as sugar. It also can greatly increase a diabetic's chances of eye damage and blindness. If you are a diabetic and are drinking alcohol several times a week, you are truly playing Russian Roulette with your health. Stop it!

Be Careful With Your Feet

For a diabetic, especially a Type I, something as simple as trimming a toe nail can have disastrous results. Diabetics have lowered resistance to infection and reduced blood flow to the feet. The result is reduced sensation in the feet. Less blood flow and sensation is a dangerous combination. The chances of infection and gangrene are enormous. That can result in amputation of the foot or an entire leg. Keep an eye on your feet. A simple blister that might be harmless to a nondiabetic could quickly become a major problem for a diabetic.

The ADA Has Free Details

You can find free information about diets from the American Diabetic Association, whose literature can usually be found in any hospital, clinic or library. As most diabetics know, doctors prefer to prescribe particular diets for particular individuals with diabetes, so you should start with whatever your doctor recommends.

By doing a little research and finding the right combination of high-carbohydrate and low-fiber diet, you can reduce your need for a doctor greatly, and you may even be able to give up your pills, needles and medication — just by eating the right foods!

Diarrhea

The thing about diarrhea is that it can be a problem within itself, or a symptom of some other disease. Those diseases could be either severe or minor. But what's certain is that whenever you experience diarrhea, your body is trying to tell you something. You may have eaten something poisonous or disagreeable; your body may be under invasion by some bacteria or virus; you may be reacting to psychological or emotional stress; or you may have a more serious disease that is causing your stool to liquefy.

Just wait

If you have simple diarrhea, all you really need to do is wait it out. This is probably the very best advise there is for treating diarrhea. Your body will probably soon correct itself. Sometimes, diarrhea can be beneficial because it represents your body's attempt to rid itself quickly of something it doesn't want, so stopping can be counter-productive.

Obviously, you don't want to let diarrhea go for more than a day or two because complications will soon add up. For one thing, you will become dehydrated, you may become feverish and your body will be sapped of strength.

Try a banana — or not

It may seem strange that something as soft, easy to digest and fiber laden as a banana could help to slow down runny stools, but the yellow fruit has been known to stop diarrhea. It doesn't work with everyone all the time, but you have nothing to lose by trying it, and if it works for you — hey! that's great. Other experts warn, however, that a banana could make things worse! Either way, it's not likely that simply eating a banana is going to do you all that much harm. It definitely is more safe than an over-the-counter remedy.

Try burnt toast

An old folk remedy for diarrhea is burnt toast. Legend has it that the carbon of burnt toast will absorb some of the agents in your stomach or intestines that is causing the problem. Like the banana remedy, this may or may not work, but it certainly will do little harm to try it once or twice.

Over-the-counter medication

It won't hurt to try an anti-diarrheal medication, but using them for an extended period of time, i.e., more than a couple of days is a very bad idea. Anti-diarrhea medication can produce serious side-effects and damage your health if you take them for too long. At any rate, if your diarrhea is lasting more than a couple of days, it's time to consider professional help.

Avoid solid foods and dehydration

When you get diarrhea, it's time to treat your digestive system with kid gloves. Don't eat any solid foods for a while, take to your bed and simply get some rest. Sometimes a little bed rest can do more for stopping diarrhea than a whole bottle of some off-the-shelf medication. But while you avoid eating, make sure you replenish your body with fluids — water and Gatorade are the best for adults (but not for infants or toddlers). The liquids coming out your backside need to be replaced quickly, or you will soon get sicker.

Is dairy your problem?

One of the most common causes of diarrhea is lactose intolerance, or the inability to properly digest dairy products. You can easily test yourself by watching your own reaction to milk, ice cream and other dairy products. If that's so, supplements are now available in drug stores that can help your body tolerate dairy products. Give them a try, but mostly you should listen to the wishes of your body. If it doesn't want milk and ice cream, don't give it any!

Other foods?

Normally, high fiber foods are just what the doctor ordered, but while you have diarrhea, they can make things worse.

Foods such as prunes, apples, just about any fruit or fruit juice, may contribute to diarrhea. Again, the best thing to do at the onset of diarrhea is to avoid eating in general, but especially avoiding high fiber stuff is important.

When to get help

If your diarrhea springs on you suddenly and severely, if you have blood in your stool, if your skin becomes yellowish or otherwise discolored, if you have bad cramps, sharp pains or any other kind of significant pain or discomfort — don't fool around, see a professional. Diarrhea which lasts too long or which is accompanied by other symptoms should not be treated lightly. Diarrhea can quickly drain away your health, weaken you considerably and lead to more serious illness.

Special Report

Dreams: The Healing Power of Our Nighttime Lives

Sleep researchers at some of America's and Europe's most prestigious universities are excited about the potential of using dreams to improve the health and heal the bodies of people.

How is this possible? How can something as wispy, confusing and seemingly meaningless as a dream have an effect on our waking lives, or do anything to manipulate or "real" physical bodies?

The idea that dreams can be used for healing is nothing new. In ancient times, seeking healing within dreams was a widespread and respected method of curing ailments. In some traditions, sick people slept inside special temples or rooms that were built for the purpose of inducing healing dreams.   More than 400 dream temples were built throughout the Greek islands and along the coast of Asia Minor.

But the fact is, modern science knows that certain hormones and the natural self-healing attributes of the physical body are triggered during sleep time, regardless of whether a person is consciously seeking healing, or just taking a snooze.

Since it has already been established that sleep has restorative and healing powers, pursueing dreaming in a more direct, pro-active way may hold exciting potential for our physical health.

Dream Healing: Where you can begin

If youwant to try your own hand at dream healing, you don't have to have a degree in psychology or advanced sleep research.   Here is a simple technique that many people have found to be incredibly powerful, both in relieving a negative mental state or a physical ailment.

When you go to bed tonight, instead of going through your normal routine of hitting the sack and concking out till morning, try this: Just after you get in bed and get comfortable, preferably lying flat on your back, give yourself this simple suggestion: "Tonight, I seek a dream that will make me feel lighter, happier and healthier when I awake in the morning." Say it to yourself out loud, (Note: If your spouse or partner finds this too corny or weird, make the affirmation to yourself silently — you don't need the upsetting controversy of a debate about this just now).

After you have made your affirmation, just let it sort of drift in your mind. Your affirmation should never be a command or a forced process. Allow yourself to have a quiet feeling of expectancy about waking up and feeling better. Don't think that you have to have some specific kind of dream, or even that you have to remember it and analyze it later. Have a feeling of trust and faith — nurture a feeling of letting go and "knowing" that some kind of process will work for you as you sleep tonight.

That's all there is to it.

The result of this may surprise you. The difference you feel when you wake up can be dramatic. If it doesn't work the first time, try again the next night. In fact, it won't hurt to give yourself the same simple dream affirmation every night for, say, a week. Keep plugging away at it. When you do achieve results, it will have been well worth the mere 10 seconds you use each night to make a pre-sleep affirmation for better health.

Dream Healing: Level Two

If you liked the results you achieved with a simple pre-sleep affirmation, perhaps you are ready to go on to using a specific dream and dream imagery to achieve healing.

First, you should take steps to increase the number of dreams you have each night, the clarity of those dreams and your ability to remember them in the morning. The best way to do this is to start a dream journal. A dream journal is simply a notebook in which you write down all the dreams you can remember from each night.

Once you start recording your dreams on paper, you will notice an immediate and remarkable increase in the number and clarity of your dreams. You want to get to the point where you have at least one dream per night that is fairly clear and easy to remember.

When you achieve a stronger ability to dream and remember them, it's time to attempt a dream of healing.

Depending on your condition or health problem, you will want to attempt to induce a specific, clear dream that focuses on your medical problem in a specific way. In your dream, you will try to influence your health problem directly. Here are a couple of examples of people who have used dream healing techniques to solve medical problems:

"I sprained my ankle in dance class, just two days before we were set to perform before a live audience in a play that was important to my career on the stage I decided to induce a dream that would speed the healing of my ankle. That night I made an affirmation before I went to sleep to heal my ankle in a dream. To my delight, I found myself in a very clear dream in which I pictured my ankle, red and swollen. Still in my dream, I walked over to a stream of beautiful, cool, crystal water and placed my ankle in. The cool water felt soothing and terrific! When I woke up the next morning, my ankle was completely healed!"

Dream Healing: Level Three

Now you can take dream healing a step further by learning to recognize the power of dream symbolism to heal your body.

As you may know, dreams are not always as clear and straightforward as the example above. Sometimes objects or concepts don't appear to us as themselves in dreams, but rather as symbols. But once you learn to recognize and interpret dream symbols, you will have at your disposal an extremely powerful tool for healing your body. Let's look at another actual case study to show how dream symbolism works:

For a long time I had been having terrible difficulty with

allergies to dust and pollens that swelled up my nose, eyes and often ended up in terrible migraine headaches. I decided to see what I could do about this by seeking a healing dream.

Before I was ready to go to sleep, I gave myself this affirmation: "Tonight I will dream about my allergy to dust and pollen, and I will help my body find a solution to it."

That night I suddenly found myself in a dream in which I was walking in a dark jungle full of cackling birds, scary dark shadows and moving shapes that were lurking behind thick foliage. I was afraid something would jump out at me at any moment and tear me to shreds. Suddenly I found a gigantic machine gun in my hands, complete with large strings of ammunition crisscross about both my shoulders, just like Rambo.
I opened fire on the woods, spraying a dreadful hail of bullets and death into the forest, hoping I would kill every harmful thing in the shadows. But instead of feeling better and more safe, I began to feel as if I was overreacting, and that using the big machine gun was causing as much terror as the forest had brought me before. I was concerned that I would be killing good animals along with the bad.

Suddenly I remembered my dream affirmation. I automatically realized that the noises and shapes I was afraid of in the woods were the symbolic representations of the dusts and pollens in the environment, and that my giant machine gun was my own overactive immune system. I put the gun down and it disappeared. After that happened, the evil shapes in the woods transformed themselves into friendly, soft cuddly animals which I was able to pet and take delight in.

When I woke up, I realized that my allergies were the result of an overactive immune system triggered by dust and pollen in the air. From that time on, I never had an allergic reaction again. The dream had helped by body chemistry make the proper adjustments, and I rarely have allergic reactions any more.

As you can see in the above example, dream healing can be quite dramatic, and does require some facility and presence of mind to stay with your dream when it gets scary or difficult. It also requires the ability for you to become lucid within your dreams, that is, to recognize the fact that you are in a dream, and that you can use your normal, waking consciousness within that framework.

Dream healing may be closely akin to the mental tools that some cancer clinics are teaching to their patients. People with cancerous lumps or other malignant conditions are taught to visualize their lumps growing smaller, or to make their body's immune system work harder to fight off the disease. Dreaming is really another form of creative visualization, but may be even more powerful because of the dream's ability to put people in a direct, super-realistic environment with their medical situation.

For more on dream healing, ask your librarian or bookstore for books by dream experts Patricia Garfield, Ph.D., or Dr. Stephen LeBerge of Stanford University.

Ear Problems

Very few people with children are not familiar with the problems of ear aches and ear infections. Some people and families are far more susceptible to earaches and repeat earaches, while others rarely have this problem.

The most common kind of ear problem is called Ostitis Media, or inflammation of the inner ear. Children get it the most, but some adults get it as well.

Most of the time earaches are the result of bacterial infection, but can also be caused by viruses or allergies. If it's a bacterial infection, the problem will likely get worse quickly and may cause hearing loss, especially in children three years old and under, so it's important to get an antibiotic treatment.

There won't always be pain associated with an ear infection, but a youngster may tug or pull on the ear a lot more than usual, tipping you off to the problem.

One of the biggest problems with ear infections is that they tend to cause problems well beyond the ear itself. Dizziness, vomiting and fainting can result from an ear infection. Associated with earaches are infections of the throat, tonsils and adenoids.

As we have said, earaches caused by bacterial infection need an antibiotic to fix them. Earaches caused by viruses — which are more common — usually fix themselves, especially if you take the proper steps to take care of the problems.

Here's what to do:

No aspirin or Tylenol!

Don't take aspirin or other pain killers, such as Tylenol! That will mask the pain. If the infection gets worse, you may not know it, causing further ear damage, and perhaps hearing loss.

Try Good ol' red flannel

An old folk remedy for earache is pressing some warm, red flannel to the ear. It will work even better if you make sure that the flannel has been warmed, with moisture or by heat lamp. While the heat may be the most effective part of the red flannel treatment, the healing power of certain colors is getting a lot of attention in some cutting-edge alternative medicine circles. The specific wavelength of the color red may have some healing properties for the ear, so warm red flannel may be just the thing you need.

To clean the ears:

• Buy an earwax cleaning solution from a drugstore, or you can use peroxide, alchohol or a solution that contains equal parts vinegar and water. Put the recommended number of drops in the ear at bedtime. If your ear is infected, apply heat for 15 minutes after the drops go in.

• Then turn your ears onto a paper towel to let them drain.
• Do this three or four times on successive days. This should clean out the ears as good as can be done without the help of a professional.

Keeping the ear canal free of wax will aid a doctor in making a diagnosis of your ear problem.

More Earache Tips

Not all earaches are the same or have the same cause. In addition to bacterial and viral infections, many other things can cause an earache in your inner or outer ear. Here are a few common sources of ear pain or infection:

•Sudden loud noise — check for bleeding, or see a doctor to examine for a ruptured ear drum

•Long-term noise (such as too much loud music) — will eventually lead to ear damage and hearing loss. Just avoid it. Use common sense. Don't blast away at your ears day after day. Do you want to be deaf some day? I think not.

•Swimming pool water — Can cause itchiness or infections. Make sure you dry out your ears after using a swimming pool. Jump up and down to get water out and use a blow dryer to dry up the insides.

•Earings — Earings made from cheap material can cause infection in pierced ears. Remove them if you feel you have that problem and don't wear rusty or low-grade metal earings. They should be at least 14K gold.

Dizziness

Dizziness can be caused by a number of medical problems, but problems with the ear are always a very possible source of vertigo, or dizziness.

Take care of the primary problem and lie down

Of course, dealing with the specific problem you are having will help your dizziness as well. If you have an infected ear and you are also feeling dizzy, it's time to lie down. The rest will help your infection, and your dizziness will be minimized. Shutting off the lights or covering your eyes will also help because you won't be able to see anything swirl around, making things worse.

A Dram is Better Than a Damn

The over-the counter drug, Dramamine, may correct your dizziness, but don't rely too heavily on this drug, especially not for more than a day or two. Dramamine restores the normal fluid balance in your ears and restores your equilibrium.

Your diet?

If your dizziness cannot be directly linked to a specific ear problem, it may be a lousy diet, or even food poisoning that is causing the problem. Once again, the high-fat, high-cholesterol diet rears its ugly head as a source of illness. In addition to all the other horrors a high-fat diet brings to your health — from heart disease to stomach cancer — too many fat molecules in your blood may be interfering with the normal oxygen levels in your blood, thus making you light-headed from 02 deprivation. If you suspect this is your problem, hit the low-fat foods, try some garlic supplements or see your doctor for a blood test and to discuss the possibility further.

Don't mix aspirin with anti-diarrhea medications

Many stomach or anti-diarrheal medication do not mix well with aspirin. Taking them together can cause ringing in the ears or dizziness. Check the label of such products as Pepto-Bismal for indications against mixing them with aspirin.

If your dizziness or earache persists over several days, if you experience increased pain or have an elevated fever, it's time to see a doctor.

Hearing Loss

If you are hearing less and less these days, there's a gigantic chance that too much exposure to noise is behind the problem. There are many sources loud, harmful noises in our every day environment — traffic, construction work, music, home appliances, power tools and more.

Even if you find most of these daily noises not especially loud, prolonged exposure to them — and combinations of sounds — can add up to dangerous, ear damaging noise in a hurry.

Use your common sense to rid your daily environment of excess noise. Turn off that darned television — better yet, toss it out the window. Don't be foolhardy with your Walkman or stereo. Get a muffler on your car and if you live next to a busy street, perhaps a move is in order. It will help you sleep better, reduce your stress and save your hearing over the long run.

Other causes of hearing loss are viral infections which can attack the inner ear structure and nerve endings in the ear. If that's the case, you need to get rid of the infections first. Most often, your hearing will slowly return if you treat them with kid gloves — that is — avoid loud, stressful noises.

Beware of swindlers

The hearing aid racket is just that — a racket. There's something about the business of selling hearing aids that brings out a lot of hucksters who want to make a fast buck either with phoney devices that do little to improve hearing, or with phoney hearing tests that tell people they have impaired hearing.

Always get a second opinion whenever you take a hearing test. And always do your homework — check consumer reports magazines and ask others about the quality of their devices — before you pay big bucks for a hearing aid.

Edema

Edema is a condition in which swelling of the ankles or

lower legs occurs because of water-retention in the body. Edema is the result in the disturbance of the fluid balance in your body, and the most serious forms of edema are the by-products of heart disease and kidney disease.

If your edema is caused by kidney or heart problems, it's important that you see a doctor to deal with this complex problem. Most likely you will have a diuretic prescribed. A diuretic is a drug that increases your rate of urination. Common beverages, such as coffee and alcohol are also diuretics, but using these may not be good for your heart or kidneys, so see what your doctor has to say about it.
Also, your swollen legs and ankles could be telling you that you have a kidney problem that you don't know about, so pay attention to what your body is trying to tell you.

An allergy?

Swelling of the legs or ankles can also be caused by an allergy. If you suspect that an allergy is causing your legs or ankles to swell, see the heading in this book under "Allergy."

Menstrual problems?

Edema is also associated with the fluid retention which some women experience during premenstrual periods. See heading under menstrual Problems for more information about how to deal with swelling and fluid retention.

Emphysema

There's probably a good chance you know someone in your life who has emphysema, or even someone who has died from it. As you know, this disease makes it very hard to breathe. Most people associate it (correctly) with smoking, but nonsmokers can develop this disease as well. Emphysema can have many causes, including repeated infections of the lungs, particularly harsh allergies or heavy and persistent exposure to dusts and pollutants.

Emphysema is actually the enlargening of the air spaces in the lungs. The air spaces enlarge because they lose their elasticity — much like a balloon that has been blown up too large, stretching the rubber until it becomes loose and placid. With emphysema, your lungs become unable to spring back to their normal state after breath inhalation. The result is a loss in useful lung volume, less oxygen to the blood and increased frequency of bronchitis.

People with emphysema are short of breath, cough a lot, have wheezing spells, are short of energy, have dizziness and have more colds and infections thatnother people.

Emphysema is a chronic condition that usually only gets worse, but there is much you can do to slow this disease and even improve the way your lungs work.

Clean up your act, clean up your surroundings

Obviously, you should remove that harmful environmental conditionwhich generated your disease in the first place. That may be dust you contact in the workplace, the heavy pollution of a crowded city — or most likely — those darned cigarettes and second-hand smoke.

Do we even have to remind you that smoking will not only greatly increase your chances of getting emphysema, but will also cause your lungs to deteriorate more rapidly and kill you sooner? It will. Believe it. Also, second hand smoke will drag you down almost as fast, so avoid it at all costs.

Use steam inhalation

Something that will really help you breath is air that is cool and moist. Especially if you live in a dry, arid climate, getting enough fresh clean air can be hard for a person with emphysema. You can create a small artificial environment for yourself no matter where you live that will give you a place to breath easy.

Create a tent for yourself by placing an open umbrella at the head of your bed, drape a sheet over it and place a cool-vapor machine inside of it. You can get a vapor machine at any drug store or health care supply store.

Lie down under your tent for 30 minutes to 1 hour two or three times a day. You can also sleep under your homemade breathing tent for the night if you wish. You'll breathe and sleep easier and wake more rested and with more energy.

Exercise

You may think that exercise is the last thing a person with emphysema should do because of all the coughing and wheezing that might ensue. But it has long been known that exercise is one of the best things for emphysema. Just as exercise increases the lung capacity and strengthens the overall health of normal people, people with emphysema can reap the same benefits with a moderate exercise program.

The best exercise for people with emphysema is light walking. While some people find it difficult to even walk across a room, you can start from wherever your current capacity is and try to improve yourself slowly. Challenge yourself. Don't give in to your disease. Exercise will help you mentally as well as physically by giving you goals to work towards and achievements to feel good about.

Space your meals

Eat small meals and take them 4 or 5 times daily. Because your lungs expand with emphysema, they will tend to crowd your stomach. Eating large meals will be more difficult and will also draw oxygen away from your lungs for the purpose of digestion.

Eat more vitamins C, E and A

Vitamin C, while good for so much else, is also associated with building stronger lungs. People who have high intakes of vitamin C show slower rates of lung deterioration. The beta-carotene content of foods high in vitamin E and A have also been linked to better lung tissue. Generally, if a food is yellow or orange, it contains generous amount of E and A. Carrots, squash, sweet potatoes, cantaloupes and so on are all excellent sources of vitamin E, A and beta-carotene. Be careful with E and A supplements, because they can have toxic side effects if you take them in too large quantities.

Take you r temperature often

It is important to monitor your temperature closely because infections of the lungs are common for people with emphysema. If temperature gets above 101, see a doctor for some antibiotics.

Maintain high fluid intake

If you keep your fluid intakes high, you will keep your bronchial secretions thinner, less harmful, easier to cough up and less likely to lead to infection.

Avoid sudden changes in temperature, and be quiet

Sudden changes in humidity and air temperature can bring on a coughing episode. Loud talking or shouting can also trigger coughing. Maintain an even keel. Be aware that even the smallest, sudden exertions could set you off, including your own, unrestrained voice.

Sleep with your head downhill

Try raising up the foot of your bed about a half-foot. Place some 5- 6-inch blocks beneath the bedposts. This will help drain any secretions during the night and leave you less congested. It will also make coughing easier and less damaging.

A breathing Exercise, or two

A breathing exercise which is often used by asthmatics can be helpful for people with emphysema. It's called pursed-lips breathing. It's simple, and here's how to do it:

Stand up straight or sit up straight in a chair, close your mouth and inhale through your nose. Purse your lips and exhale slowly through your nose. Count as you exhale and exhale for twice as long as you inhale. For example, if you breathe in for five seconds, try breathing out for 10 seconds.

Don't hold your breath between inhaling and exhaling. Stop if pursed lip breathing makes you dizzy or light-headed.

Try to do the exercise twice each minute. Relax in between the exercise.

Abdominal breathing:

Here's another way of breathing that can help:

While lying flat on the floor on your back, put your right hand on your stomach and your left hand on your chest. While slowly inhaling, push out your stomach (make yourself look like a pregnant woman) and let your right hand rise visibly. Then exhale through pursed lips and slowly press your stomach toward your backbone.

You can repeat this exercise while slowly raising and lowering your legs, one at a time, to strengthen your abdominal muscles.

Remember your mind

Emphysema is one of those diseases that requires perhaps a special mental adjustment on your behalf to help you cope and live with the disease.

It's true that there is no current cure for emphysema and that life as you have always known it will never be the same. But the longer you reject the reality of that, you will squander energy uselessly on guilt, regrets and depression.

Stop blaming yourself. Even if you brought on the disease with too much smoking, heaping loads of guilt and regret on yourself is absolutely counter-productive. Accept your situation, but don't resign to it. Acknowledge what you have done in the past, but now let it go. Ask yourself what you are going to do today to improve the quality of your life, and to make sure you have the longest, most normal life you can have.

Making the mental adjustment to emphysema is just as important as the physical steps you take to improve your lot in life. Work on the attitude thing, and you'll be doing everything you can to live with one of the greatest challenges life can hand out to a person.

Energy Depletion

It just seems like you never have enough energy. You drag yourself from one end of your day to the next like a semi-comatose zombie. Three cups of coffee to you are about as stimulating as a glass of warm milk combined with soft music. Your sleep is a black hole of nothingness that leaves you just as tired after eight hours as you were when you hit the pillow the night before. Your mind feels slow, you are mildly depressed, you just can't seem to get your act together.

On the other hand, you feel there is nothing particularly wrong with you. You're not sick, you get enough sleep, you life is relatively normal and boring — so why do you feel so tired all the time?

Chronic fatigue or energy depletion is one of those amorphous conditions that could have its origin in some quite obvious deficiencies of your life, or it could be something hidden and hard to pinpoint. It may also be a combination of factors.

Be Your Own P.I.

Think of your search for more energy as a detective story. You are going to act as your own private investigator, searching out clues, eliminating false leads, and eventually solving the mystery of your fatigue, leaving you a more healthy, happy, energized, vibrant person.

Where to start

Perhaps the best way to start is to first make sure that you really do have a clean bill of health. It's probably way past time you had a complete physical anyway, so you might as well make an appointment for a blood test and a quick exam by a qualified doctor or physician's assistant.

You want to rule out some of the most common diseases that are associated with chronic fatigue — anemia, diabetes, hypoglycemia and others. It will be an easy matter to rule these out, and just knowing that you don't have a more serious condition should lift your spirits and make you realize that there is probably something simple you can do to increase your energy level.

Take a look at the obvious things

Now that you have ruled out a major medical condition, you can take a serious examination of your daily life and habits to see if anything you are doing consciously or unconsciously is sapping your strength.

Your diet? — This seems so obvious it almost seems ludicrous for us to point it out to you, but maybe your diet isn't all it should be. Even if you think you have fairly good eating habits, a closer examination may surprise you. The best way to get a handle on just what you are eating is to keep a daily log of every single thing you eat and drink. Carry around a small notebook with you and record everything that goes in your mouth and how often. Write down everything from chewing gum to that major 6-course meal. After two weeks, take a close look at what's been going into your system.

Ever hear that saying, "Garbage in, garbage out?" If you are eating garbage — lots of fatty meats, lots of sugar, lots of empty-calorie foods, such as sweet rolls and white bread, lots of alcohol and diet soda — then you are probably going to feel like garbage. It's that simple.

Make sure that your diet is balanced and contains a greater proportion of fruits, vegetables and fiber than it does meat, fat, cholesterol and empty, simple carbohydrates.

Could it be as simple as that? A new diet and a new energized life — absolutely so! Albert Einstein once said, "it takes a genius to see the obvious." Why not see the obvious in your own life? Life doesn't always have to be so complex and hidden. Try a few simple things, like a healthier diet, and see what happens.

What you drink?

You know that alcohol is a depressant and that it is basically a poison to your system. It does nothing to make you feel energized. Even if you drink very little, just a couple of drinks in one day can ruin your life for several days. It's true. Some people are so sensitive to alcohol that just a drink or two will slow their body down for a week or more. Your liver hates alcohol, and it also feeds harmful bacteria, such a yeast cells in your intestines. A properly functioning liver and digestive system is vital to your energy level. Keep alcohol away from it — totally — and see what happens.

How about coffee? It's a stimulant you say — it will pick me up. Well, it could be doing exactly the opposite in the long run. No one denies that coffee is a strong stimulate in the short term, but coffee is also a diuretic, which means it makes you urinate more. As your urination increases, your body is depleted of vital nutrients it needs to run properly and feel awake. Specifically, potassium and B vitamins are depleted by too much coffee drinking, and both of those are linked powerfully to your level of energy. So remember, coffee will give you a quick jolt, but as it gives, it also takes away.

Many soft drinks are no better than coffee. Did you know that one can of Pepsi has nine teaspoons of dissolved sugar in it? Coke has seven teaspoons of sugar in each can. Try eating nine teaspoons of white sugar once and then tell me how you feel. You'd be sick, buzzed and depressed all at once, right? Well, every time you drink a can of just about any soft drink, you are literally shoveling sugar into your mouth and paying the consequences. Diet sodas are not much better because they contain caffeine — a diuretic — and you're back to same problem as coffee.

Just drink water or fruit juice all day, and, Hey!, your energy levels may jump up to a maximum high in just a few days.

Exercise

Once again, this seems so obvious that it almost seems preachy to mention it. But the amount of exercise you get, or don't get, has a strong influence on your general level of energy. If you are a couch potato, then your body will feel like a couch potato — that is — like a dead lump of starch fit for nothing but laying around and getting baked.

To keep your level of energy up, you must exercise for at least 30 minutes, three or four times a week. If you're not doing that now, don't come whining to us. You now what you have to do. Come on! Move it!

Sleeping Problems?

What about sleeping problems? If you can't sleep at night, obviously you won't be awake and refreshed in the morning and during the following day. Even if you think you are sleeping soundly, you may not be. For example, if you drink too much coffee, the caffeine will disturb your sleep even if you never wake up. The same with loud noises or other distractions. Even if they never wake you up, they make your sleep more shallow and less productive. Soo the heading under "Insomnia" for a 10-point sleeping program that will make sure you are getting the quality sleep you need.

Sleeping too much can also make you more tired during the following day. Sleeping too long can lead to fragmented, shallow sleep that doesn't do you any good.

Don't forget snoring. People who snore a lot can easily suffer from a lack of oxygen to their brain at night. Snoring involves swallowing your tongue and partially blocking the air that's going down your windpipes. Less oxygen to the brain means more sleepiness.

Now the not-so-obvious

When you have eliminated the obvious, such as a serious illness, bad daily habits or poor sleep — and you still feel groggy and run down — it's time to dig a little deeper to get to the bottom of this.

Pills or poisons?

Maybe something you are taking for a medical condition or something you are coming into contact with in your environment is running you down.

If you take any medicine regularly — even aspirin — consider the possibility that it may be causing your fatigue. If you have a lot of headaches that you like to treat with aspirin or Tylenol a side effect may be fatigue. As you know, aspirin thins your blood. If you take it often enough, it may be sapping your energy.

Ask your doctor about any drug he has prescribed for you, even if it something you apply only to the surface of your skin. Fatigue is a common side-effect of many prescription drugs.

And what about your house? Do you have a wood stove or

a fireplace? Do you know that burning wood produces carbon monoxide as a by-product? Even a small amount of carbon monoxide in your house can make you fuzzy. If you have a wood stove or a fireplace, keep a crack in a window open to ensure that enough fresh oxygen is getting into your house. The same goes for your car, especially if you have an older model. Driving with the windows up tight in the winter can raise the carbon monoxide level in your car. It could make you tired while you are driving and for the rest of the day. Always crack the window a bit.

Another source of carbon monoxide is cigarettes and their second-hand smoke. Smoking or breathing someone else's smoke can make you very lethargic and even cause depression.

Carbon monoxide is only one of many toxins we come into contact with in our daily lives. Gasoline fumes, glue, pesticides or herbicides can all have an adverse affect ofnyour general level of energy. Do you have frequent or even moderate contact with any of these? Any one could be the culprit.

In general, check out everything you eat and your total environment for any chemical or poison that may be creeping its way into your life.

Maybe you have SAD

SAD stands for Seasonal Affective Disorder. It's a form of depression and fatigue that strikes people in the winter when there is less sunshine. Lack of sunshine has a depressing effect on the body chemistry of some people. The cure for SAD is to get more sun. The way to get more sun is to take a vacation down south, or buy an artificial lamp that provides the same range of light radiation that the real sun provides. For more about SAD, see heading under "Depression."

Psychological Factors?

A general lack of energy and feeling of tiredness could simply mean you are depressed. If you are, then you have a whole other realm of factors to consider. Rather than go into the complex processes of depression here, turn to the section in this book under "Depression" and go from there.

There may be other psychological factors — simple or complex — that are behind your lack of energy. If you think you have thoroughly and carefully ruled out physical problems, then perhaps it's time to explore your mental and emotional life to see if there's anything there that's keeping you down. Is it a particular problem you just can't face? A bad marriage? Something you did a long time ago you feel guilty about?

The possibilities are endless, but don't be daunted. Just the fact that you have committed yourself to a search for answers within yourself can be an energizing process. In taking up a personal journey through your own soul, you may find that the journey itself is the very thing you needed all along to move your life forward in a positive and energetic way.

The possibility of CFS — Chronic Fatigue Syndrome

If all else fails, consider the possibility that you have Chronic Fatigue Syndrome (CFS). Many doctors now believe that CFS is a specific disease with a specific cause. Although surrounded by myths, controversy, doubts and heresay for years, CFS is increasingly being taken seriously as clearly defined disease.

The problem with CFS is that its symptoms can be attributed to so many other things in life, many of which we have talked about above in our discussion about low energy.

Also, since there is no known cause of cure for CFS, treating it as you would any other normal long-term fatigue will be very helpful.

Getting a positive diagnosis of CFS means you need to see a doctor and undergo a lot of tests. You will have to decide for yourself if you want to take this route — it all depends on how bad or entrenched your condition is and how much it is disrupting your life.

Don't make the mistake, however, of writing off all your problems to the fact that you may have some kind of mysterious disease, such as CFS. If you really suspect you have CFS, then see a doctor to take care of it. In the meantime, take a sober look at your total lifestyle — from your diet to your conscience — and face whatever you see bravely.

Eye Problems

The eyes are one of nature's most magnificent inventions. The eyes draw the blissful light of the world into your consciousness where you make of it what you will — triumph or tragedy, beauty or horror, pain or pleasure, delight or disgust.

The eye is a tenuous, delicate instrument. Of all your five senses, who would not be the first to admit that sight is the most precious. Of course, blind people learn to live happily without it, but given the choice, they would choose to see the light.

Many eye problems require the expertise of a professional.

On the other hand, there are many common eye problems you can deal with yourself, and there are many things you can do to avoid serious eye problems.

Cataracts

These filmy, white coverings which grow over the eyes of mostly elderly people used to be a very serious problem that required surgery. Nowadays, cataracts are removed by surgery long before they get thick and before they significantly disrupt your vision. But before you get to the point where surgery becomes necessary, there is much you can do to prevent cataracts from developing in the first place.

Avoid too much sun

Ultraviolet light from the sun is now believed to lead to the deposit of certain pigments in your eye lenses. Always wear a shady hat and UV protective sunglasses to shield your eyes from harmful sun radiation.

Aspirin and some "C" for clarity?

Many doctors recommend that people with high risk of heart disease take an aspirin a day to reduce their chances of heart attack. There is now some evidense to suggest that aspirins may also prevent cataracts. If you can tolerate aspirin, it may be okay for you to take one day for your general health. Ask your doctor before you start yourself on aspirin, though. If you have a weak stomach or an ulcer, or if you are asthmatic, aspirin is definetly not for you.

Vitamin C, which seems able to fix everything from aging to emphysema has also been named as an anti-cataract agent. Take a couple of vitamin C tablets a day — it will help you with all sorts of things, including your eyesight.

No smoking

Smoking seems to be the very antithesis of vitamin C. While vitamin C provides incredibly far-reaching health benefits for your body, smoking inflicts an incredible number of ills on the same. Cataracts may be one of them. If you smoke, you are increasing your chances of needing eye surgery some day.

Eye Redness and Itching

Think of all the things that feel like sawdust on your eyes — smoke, pollution haze, dusty wind on a hot day, chaff from grain, a cold, dry January wind glaring sunlight or a bright welder's flame — and many more.

Many things can irritate your eyes, but making them feel better is very easy. And you don't need to go out an spend your hard-earned dollars on the eye solutions advertised on TV. They do nothing for your eyes that a simple moist washcloth won't also do.

To treat burning, itching red eyes, simply moisten a washcloth, lie down and place it across your eyes. The coolness of the water will shrink the tiny blood vessels in your eyes, reducing redness and providing a soothing feeling. The moisture of the washcloth will also add to the moisture you have lost from your eye, which is why it feels the way it does.

Eyestrain

This is different from redness and itching because it has different causes. Eyestrain is the result of using your eyes in difficult situations, such a squinting against bright lights, trying to read print that is too small, looking into a computer screen all day and other light sources.

Have your eyes checked to make sure you don't need glasses. Even if you don't, it may help you to use reading glasses which make print bigger if you have to do a lot of reading all day.

Remember to provide shade for your eyes while you work if you can. If you work on a computer all day, adjust the screen appropriately so the brightness and color are easy on your eyes.

An exercise for eyestrain

Here's something that will "loosen up" your eyes, make them stronger and be more resistent to eye strain.

Look at a small object up close so that it requires you to focus your eyes as closely as you can. Once you see the tiny thing clearly, look away to a distant object. You will feel you eyes refocusing. The muscles that are used for this process are being exercised when you do this. Repeat the procedure several times a day, and do it vice versa. It's a good one-two workout for the eyes and will give them a stretch and a lift.

The juice of an orange peeling

In many parts of India, it is believed that the sour, acidic juice that can be squeezed from an orange peeling is very beneficial for your eyes. Next time you eat an orange, zap your eyes a bit with a tiny bit of orange-peel juice. You'll feel a teeny sting, but it does have a refreshing effect on the eyes.

Bags beneath your eyes — tea bags, that is

Tea leaves contain tannin, a natural astringent that can make skin swell slightly making it feel a bit tighter for a short time. This can relieve puffiness of your eyes. Be careful, though. Tea could also stain your skin around your eyes — which may not be exactly the look you're after.

The eye press

Here's an excellent acupressure treatment to relieve sore, tired and strained eyes:

Rub around the boney orbits of both eyes using medium pressure applied with the middle fingers. Begin at the inner corners of the eyes and move first along the lower orbit toward the temples. Do this in about 15 seconds. Then begin again at the inner corners and move along the upper part of the orbit toward the temples. Do the lower and upper orbits twice each.

More serious eyes diseases

One of the best known and serious eye diseases is glaucoma. Glaucoma is caused by pressure on the eyes resulting from the build-up of eye fluids which normally drain away.

If left untreated, glaucoma will blind you. Onset of glaucoma is characterized by headaches, seeing halos around light sources, blurred vision and rapidly declining eyesight.

Only a doctor can treat glaucoma. Don't fool around if you suspect you have it. Get it fixed before you go blind.

Pink Eye or Conjunctivitis

Pink Eye, more properly known as conjunctivitis, is an inflammation of the outside mucus covering of the eye. It involves pink streaks over the eye's surface. It is usually caused by viral or bacterial infection, but also can result from severe and persistent eyestrain. Pink Eye can also accompany colds and flu.

People who develop conjunctivitis may wake up with eyes so sticky they are stuck shut in the morning. Eyes are also hypersensitive to light and there may be blurred vision. Sticky discharge is a strong clue that you actually have conjuntivitis.

Pink eye is contagious! be careful not to transfer it to everyone in your family. Wash your hands, don't share a towel and avoid direct contact.

Here's what else you can do:

(1) Apply a warm, wet compress to the eye four times a day.

(2) Avoid constant wiping of the eye and lid because it will cause chapping.

(3) Aspirin will ease pain.

(4) Do not use a bandage or an eye patch.

(5) Wear sunglasses for protection.

(6) If you don't get better in 24 hours, see a doctor.

Styes

These are infected infections around the root of an eyelash. They sometimes require antibiotics from your doctor, but they can also be treated with warm compresses, much the same as for Pink Eye described above. If that doesn't work and the stye persists or gets bigger, get thee to a doctor.

Iris inflammation — a simple test

Do you have a red, irritated eye you suspect is infected? Here's a simple test you can use to get a handle on the problem:

Cover your affected eye with your hand and then flash a brief light into the other eye. If pain occurs in the covered eye it means that the iris is inflamed. If that's the case, it's time for a doctor.

Macular Degeneration — a simple test

Macular degeneration most often attacks people over 50. It starts when the small blood vessels of the eyes become restricted, cutting off blood supply to the retina. The blood vessels can also burst or leak. The result is blurred or obstructed central vision and eventual blindess for many.

Here is a simple test for macular degeneration:

Cover one eye with your hand and stare at a long straight line, such as a door frame. If the line appears bent or twisted, or a black spot gets in the way, you are on your way to a case of macular degeneration and it's time to see a doctor.

Crossed eyes

Newborn babies can sometimes develop crossed eyes, which usually goes away after six months. If one eye continues to wander, a condition known as amblyopia may have developed. In this case, the child may need corrective lenses or surgery to correct the muscles of one eye or both.

Injury to the eyes

Stable-eyes

An eye injury can be tough to deal with because attempts to help can lead to further damage and blindness.

If a sharp or protruding object — such as a pencil or piece of glass — becomes lodged in the eye, it's vital that you do not try to pull it out or move it around! In this case, immobalizing the object until you get to an emergency room is the best thing to do. The best way to do that is to place a styrofoam cup over the entire eye, if it will fit over the object, and stabilize it with bandages. If you can't do that, try to wrap the offending object as carefully as possible — without moving it — so that it can't move and cause further damage to the eye.

Sometimes removing the bottom of a styrofoam cup makes a good covering around the eye to keep it protected and to stabalize a protruding object.

Flush and Fold

Small objects, such as specks, can be removed by pulling your top eyelid over onto your bottom lid. Flushing the eye before you do this may help, if not get rid of the speck altogether.

If flushing and folding over the lid doesn't work, get someone to touch a cloth or paper towel to the object — ever so gently — which usually results in removal of the object.

And Finally ... eat for your eyes

It is well-known folklore that carrots are good for your eyes. Guess what? The folklore is true. All foods with red or orangish tints contain high amount of vitamin A and beta-carotene, both vital nutrients for proper eyesight. Include carrots in your diet, and you'll be giving your eyes what they need for top performance.

Fever

Like many other problems, such as coughing, diarrhea or fatigue, a fever is not a disease in itself. You never have a fever without something in your body that's causing it — and that could be any one of a hundred things.

Like diarrhea or vomiting, fever is a defense mechanism of your body. It's an attempt by your body to kill invading organisms by literally cooking them to death. It follows, then, that a fever is not all that bad. A fever makes you feel sick, but sometimes that's okay for a while. Remember, it's just your body trying to do its job.

The problems start when a fever lasts too long. That's not good for your body, but perhaps more importantly, it's a sign that whatever is causing the fever is not getting any better. The best way to treat a fever is not to try make it come down as fast as possible with aspirin or ice water on the head, but to get to the root of the problem and fix it.

When to treat a fever

Even though a fever can help kill invading organisms in your body, a fever that is too high, especially in children, can cause damage of all its own. When a fever gets to 103 or more, it's time to take steps to bring it down. If you don't, it can cause convulsions, heart problems and other complications.

What's better — aspirin or Tylenol?

Most doctors agree that Tylenol, which contains

acetaminophen, works better on a fever than does aspirin. Acetaminophen works directly on the part of your brain that regulates body temperature. Acetaminophin causes less stomach irritation than aspirin in most people, it does not thin the blood, and does not irritate asthmatic people, who should always avoid aspirin.

Other common pain killers, such as Nuprin, Advil or Motrin are also not as effective as Tylenol in treating a fever.

If a fever is "way high"

When a fever starts to get into the 104 and 105 range, you need to do more than just take pills to bring it down. A cold bath or wipe-down with cold water will help bring the overheated body under control. If a high fever persists, it's time to get to an emergency room before serious injury or death results.

Flatulance

Did you know that in some Oriental countries if you don't let a great big ... er, fart ... after a meal, the host and hostess will be tremendously insulted? A loud, public display of intestinal gas in some cultures is very important and a sign of respect and honor.

But here in the West, being gassy is something we hide at all costs in polite company.

Your body doesn't care about polite company, however. Whenever your body wants to pass gas, you either have to hold it back, let it go quietly, or find some place private to relieve the pressure.

You know the foods

One of the problems with flatulance is that many of the high-fiber foods that are extremely healthy for you also have gas as a by-product. Beans are the best example. Fortunately, you can have your beans and silence too. Perhaps the newest and best quick fix is a product called Bean-o, which you can buy in any health food store. Bean-o comes in a small bottle and just a couple of drops mixed with your gaseous food will prevent future problems.
Another option is to soak beans before you prepare them. This can wash away the gases in them before they go down the throat and, later, out the other end.

Get used to a high-fiber diet

One of the reasons many people get excessive gas from beans and many fruits and vegetables is that they are unaccustomed to the large amount of fiber these foods supply. Really, you should have more of these foods in your diet on a daily basis for proper digestion and good stomach and colon health. By eating more high fiber foods on a regular basis, you will greatly reduce your adverse reaction to them. When you get to the point where a large helping of three-bean casserole gives you no problem, you can pat yourself on the back for maintaining a healthy high-fiber diet which your body will love.

Swallowing air

There are many ways in which you may be swallowing air that is contributing to your gassiness. Here are some pointers on how to swallow less air:

• Eat more slowly

• Don't use a straw when you drink

• Stop smoking
• Avoid carbonated drinks
• Don't suck on candies or chewing gum because they make you swallow much more, and thus, swallow more air.

Foot Odor

This might seem like a minor medical issue to you, but the embarrassment of foot odor can have profound social and psychological effects on your life. If people move away from you quickly in public, or switch seat in a movie theater or bus, your feet may be isolating you from a normal public life.

The shoe-covered foot is a prime site for that odorous combination of sweat and bacteria. Considering the fact that your foot has more that 3,000 sweat glands per square foot! — odds are that foot odor can strike anyone 'at any time.

Fortunately, there are many good, easy ways to control this common problem, which also can lead to athlete's foot. The American Orthopaedic Foot and Ankle Society offers these tips:

*   Change shoes as well as socks every day, and avoid nylon socks or plastic shoes.

*   Wear thick, soft cotton socks to draw moisture away from the feet.

*   Use a mild soap and lukewarm (not hot) water to bathe feet daily.

*   Dust your feet frequently with non-medicated baby

powder or foot powder.

Gall bladder and Gallstones

Your gall bladder is a hollow, pear-shaped organ located beneath the liver in the right upper portion of the abdomen. Its function is to store and concentrate bile, a yellow fluid secreted by the liver into the intestinal tract. Bile contains chemicals which aid digestion, especially fatty foods.

The trouble usually starts when you eat too many fatty foods, especially cholesterol-rich foods, which can lead to a build-up of fats which harden and turn into "stones." These gallstones can be the size of a small seed, and can get as big as a lemon! If one of these stones become lodged in the duct that leads from the gall bladder to the intestine, you get the tremendous pain of a gallstone attack.

The result can be intense pain, nausea, fever, jaundice, bloating, belching and intolerance to fatty or spicy foods.

For many people, gallstone attacks start slowly with just a twinge of pain shortly after a big meal. The pain builds through the day. You try sitting in various positions, but none make you comfortable; you struggle with your breathing because each breath hurts; you try to lie down but find that being on your back hurts as much as anything; you try stretching — but nothing works.

As the pain builds and builds, you wonder what will happen to you, when suddenly, the pain is gone and you feel completely fine. You feel tremendous relaxation and relief and then fall asleep.

What has happened is that a gallstone has been working its way through your bile duct. When it finally passes through, your pain is gone, seemingly by a miracle. But it's not a miracle because it's only a matter of time before the pain happens again. That could be the next day, or 10 months from now.

In addition to stones, the lining of the gall bladder itself can become inflamed or infected if the cholesterol content of the bile gets too high.

Gallstones are a very common illness in America where the diet favors high-cholesterol, fatty foods. One particular group that gets gallstones more than others are Native Americans, especially Indians of the desert southwest. The reason may be the high sugar and fat content in the diet of these people.

Prevention is the best remedy

Maintaining a low-cholesterol, low-fat, low-sugar high-fiber diet will strongly reduce your chances of ever developing a gallstone or gall bladder infection. The benefits of such a diet go well beyond prevention of gallstones — cutting out the fat, sugar, and cholesterol from your diet can change your entire life, both mentally and physically.

If you think you have a gallstone

How you know? Well, you will likely have attacks of intense pain on your right side, just beneath your bottom rib. But be aware that gallstone pain can feel like it's in your back, and it can make your entire torso feel tight and bloated. You may experience belching and nausea and your skin can take on a yellowish tinge.

You can avoid gallstone attacks by avoiding greasy, fat-laden foods. Pumping cholesterol into your bloodstream is the very thing that will set the bile in your bladder a-rockin'. But if your stone is big enough, you may need surgery to take it out. To get around surgery, some hospitals are using "vibration therapy" to disintegrate your stone with sound waves, but this treatment is not widely available or wholly proven as of yet. Drugs are also sometimes used for gall bladder problems, but you need a doctor for a prescription.

Resrict fats and try garlic

As you avoid fats, you can take steps to reduce your cholesterol level. Eating a garlic clove daily, or taking garlic supplements can fight off cholesterol levels quickly. Increasing your intake of calcium and potassium will also knock back cholesterol. Turn to the section on "Cholesterol" for many more tips on how to kick your cholesterol levels down, and thus reduce your problems with gall bladder and gallstones.

Gout

A huge swollen toe or, a swollen ankle may be a form or arthritis called gout. Perhaps the most famous sufferer from this extremely painful condition was Benjamin Franklin, who could only stand for only short periods when he and the other Founding Fathers were drafting and debating the Constitution of the United States.

Gout is caused by high levels of uric acid in your blood stream, which may be the result of kidney disease or certain forms of leukemia. Unlike more common kinds of arthritis, such as rheumatoid or osteoarthritis, gout can strike suddenly and then go away again for good, although the predisposition remains with the victim forever.

Gout is probably one of the most painful afflictions you can ever experience because of razor-like crystals which form in the blood stream and collect in a joint, almost always the big toe. Gout is far more common in males. Gout can be so painful that even a bedsheet draped over an inflamed toe is too much to handle.

The bad news: There's no cure

To date, medical science has found no cure for the painful affliction of gout. There are many medications which can reduce the pain and swelling, but the predisposition to experience gout stays forever, even though some experience gout only once or twice.

The only sure way to get a proper diagnosis of gout is a blood test that will reveal the levels of uric acid in your system. But there is much you can do to prevent future attacks of gout.

The good news: Have more sex

Yes, the more orgasms you have, the less likely you are to have an attack of gout. Having an orgasm decreases the amount of uric acid in the blood of men. So get busy!

Avoid Purines and Diuretics

Drugs or beverages which increase the rate of urination also increase the level of uric acid in your blood. Two of the most common diuretic beverages are coffee and alcholic drinks. If you have a predisposition to gout, drinking a lot of coffee, beer or other alcohol is flirting with disaster.

Another chemical associated with gout is something called purine, which also raises the level of uric acid in your blood. Foods high in purines are anchovies, meat, and animal organs, such as kidneys, liver, brains, sweetbreads and minced meats. Some vegetables, such as asparagus and mushrooms, also raise uric acid levels.

Don't take aspirin for pain

Yes, aspirin will make things much worse in the case of gout. Aspirin not only interferes with some gout medications, but also slows the rate of uric acid reduction in your body. Use non-aspirin drugs instead, like Tylenol.

A cold pack can ease the pain

Put some ice on it, but remember, gout is usually so painful that even a puff of air can cause pain. You may need to immerse the toe in cold, icy water, rather than slap a pack on it. Ice will also reduce swelling and pain.

Headaches

At least 40 million Americans suffer chronic, recurrent headaches and spend $40 billion a year on medications. Migraine sufferers alone account for 65 million workdays lost each year.

One of the most common kinds of headaches is the tension headache, which accounts for about 90 percent of all headaches. Tension headaches involve continued contractions of head and neck muscles. Another common variety are vascular headaches, which involve changes in the pressure of blood vessels serving the head. Migraines are vascular. You know what a migraine feels like — throbbing pain, usually on one side of the head. It can make you feel sick all over, and can also cause you to vomit, feel woozy and dizzy.

A third kind of headache can be the result of some other disease which has nothing to do with muscle tension or vascular movement.

Migraine headaches are particularly difficult to treat because the process causing the headache changes throughout the course of the event. Blood vessels that first constrict may soon expand again. If you take a drug to make your vessels expand, it may be the last thing you need in a minute or two.

But you don't have to surrender completely to your fate if you are a migraine sufferer. Here are some time-tested and also new ways to deal with your pounding head.

Migraine headaches

Avoid red wine

Researchers believe that certain chemicals found in alcohol block an enzyme in our bodies which protects us from headaches. The chemicals in question are especially prevalent in red wine. White wine and brandy contain fewer of the enzyme blockers and gin and vodka contain almost none. Avoiding red wine will help you avoid a headache, but it's also likely that avoiding all alcohol would be a good idea too.

Try some coffee with sugar in it

Caffeine in coffee is a drug which can shrink blood vessels in your cranium. If your headache is being caused by dilated blood vessels, this may really help. On the other hand, blood vessels which dilate may quickly contract on their own, rendering the caffeine treatment ineffective. Adding sugar to your coffee may give you a quick fix to low blood sugar — a common cause of migraines. But after your coffee, you should eat something more substantial to raise your blood sugar count for more permanent headache relief.

A vinegar or lemon peel compress

Legend has it that putting a vinegar soaked cloth on your forehead will cure a headache, and there's probably some truth to it. The reason is that vinegar has a pungent odor and will also irritate the skin on your forehead. The combination of the odor in your nose and the minor irritation on your head may re-direct your pain sensitivity to the attractive forces in front of your head and in your nose.

The same goes for lemon juice or the white part of a lemon peel. The sharp odor of a lemon combined with the tingle of the acidic juice on your forehead skin can redirect your attention and pain sensitivity to these sources. Give it a try.

Ice packs

Another way to constrict the blood vessels in your head is by application of cold. You should try to get the entire top part of your head covered with either ice or gel packs. This may be most effective when you feel your headache coming on. Remove the ice when you feel better, because your blood vessels will likely soon restrict on their own and the cold may end up causing you even more of a headache.

Don't take "the pill"

Taking oral contraceptive can be dangerous for women who also suffer from migraine headaches, or they may be causing the problem altogether.

Yoga exercises

When you feel a headache coming on, find a place to lie

down. Breath deeply and relax for a few minutes. The sit up straight in a chair. Turn your head to put your chin on your right shoulder, hold it for a minute, then put it on you left shoulder for another minute. Then relax. Then put your chin on your chest, then arch back to look up at the ceiling.

Another very effective headache stretch goes like this: Sit up straight in a chair. Put your chin on your right shoulder. Put your left hand on your chin and your right hand on the back of your head. Then — gently — press your head downward, with your head still turned to the right. In other words, you want to stretch your neck while your head is turned. Do the same thing with your chin on your left. Be careful! Use common sense — don't force your head down to the point of injury. All we're after here is a gentle stretch.

You can follow this up with a few more yogic exercises of your choice. Anything that makes you stretch and breath and loosen up your neck and spinal column may very well head off your headache.

A great remedy for some — sex

A headache is usually the excuse not to make love, but doing so may chase that old headache away. Research has shown that a small number of people can find headache relief after orgasm, although masturbation and sex without orgasm does little to fix an aching head. You should really try this migraine remedy ... you really should.

Avoid high sodium food or MSG

A lot of people notice a headache after eating Chinese food or after eating TV dinners and fast food, especially hot dogs. The cause may be the high sodium content in all of the above. Check labels for sodium or MSG and avoid any with a high content. Remember, meat products, such as hot dogs, bacon and luncheon meats usually are screamingly high in sodium and nitrates. They may taste good, but your head may feel bad after.

Tension headaches

Treating the more common tension headache usually requires a different strategy from migraines. With a migraine headache, it's primarily the veins you are dealing with, but with tension headaches it is the muscles and tendons around your head and neck. Your are trying to get them to relax, loosen up and to stop creating a biological vice for your head.

Heating

Common sense tells you that if you have tight, constricted muscles anywhere in your body, a source of warmth and heat will help loosen and comfort those muscles. Applying a heating pad to the back of your neck, or sitting in a hot bath with your eyes closed will loosen you up all over, and may quickly chase your headache away.

Get a massage

If you've been battling a tension headache all day, or if you feel one coming on, there's nothing like a good neck rub or body massage to release it all. The power of human touch has already been shown to be so beneficial for so many other reasons. It is a very powerful weapon against tension headaches.

Aspirin

Aspirin may be useless for a migraine, but it can be a great help for a tension headache. Aspirin is an anti-inflammatory and can reduce minor swelling which may result from craning your neck or sitting at your desk all day.

Many people find nonaspirin drugs, such as Tylenol or Ibuprofin, ineffective against headaches, while others think they're great. But if you can tolerate aspirins, it's likely they will do a better job on head pain than the others. Some aspirin preparation, such as Anacin, also contain caffeine, which can help constrict blood vessels in your cranium if that is contributing to your tension headache.

Remember ...

While most headaches are of the common tension variety and most of the rest are vascular or migraine headaches, your headaches could be the sign of another illness — anything from ear infection to some sort of systemic illness that affects your entire body chemistry. If the conventional headache remedies don't work, maybe it's time to dig deeper via a doctor, or to ask yourself how the rest of your body feels both during your headache and all the time.

Heart Attacks and Diseases

In ancient times, people believed that the heart was the center of a person's mind, intelligence, emotions and soul. Today, we still use terms like "a broken heart," "heartache," or "good hearted" to describe personal feelings, or someone's character.

After the seat of human consciousness was shifted to the brain, the heart was demoted to the status of "pump" and plumbing, although a very important pump.

Today, the right or wrong way we treat that mighty pump in the middle of our chest makes the difference between life and death, or a healthy life and a weak, sickly life.

Also, an unhealthy heart can strike you dead suddenly. Heart attacks kill more than a half-million people in United States every year — that's 10 times the number of U.S. soldiers killed during the entire Vietnam War.

Furthermore, most people who suffer heart attacks die within two hours after it happens, so doing something about it quickly can make the difference between life and death.

Heart Attacks — What to do

The first thing to be aware of are the symptoms which precede most heart attacks. They are:

nausea	cold or clammy skin
chest pain	breathing difficulty
pain in left arm	irregular heartbeat

Another sign of impending heart attack may be swelling of the ankles (edema), shortness of breath during mild exercise, such as climbing stairs, or a certain kind of coughing that comes on when you are lying down, but stops when you stand up.

The problem with recognizing these symptoms is that many people attribute them to the wrong causes, such as stomach problems, indigestion, smoker's cough or something else. But if you are in a high-risk category for heart problems (overweight, hypertension, high cholesteral, high stress, lots of cigarettes, etc.) then quick action should be taken when at the onset of the above symptoms.

The only quick action to take is to get to a doctor as soon as possible. Remember, all heart attack fatalities happen within the first hour or two. Get to a hospital before then and your survival chances increase dramatically.

Some tips on recognizing a heart attack

(1) Any pain that has its center below the nipples is rarely a heart attack.

(2) Pain located completely on the left side of your chest is less likely to be a heart attack.

(3) If the pain is dull, then it may be a heart attack. If the pain is sharp, then it probably is not.

(4) If pain is steady and dull, it may be a heart attack; if it comes and goes, it probably is not.

(5) Is their nausea associated with your chest pain? Then it may be a heart attack.

(6) If pain lasts only a few seconds, it is not likely a heart attack. Pain that lasts up to five minutes, then resides, is more likely to be angina.

(7) Does the pain shoot into your left arm? Then it may be a real heart attack.

(8) Are you sweating, feeling clammy and having trouble breathing? Then you may be having a heart attack.

(9) If you are more comfortable lying down, then you may not be having a heart attack.

(10) If any or your pains last longer than 15 minutes, get to a doctor.

Preventing a heart attack

Better than taking quick action to deal with a heart attack is doing everything you can to prevent one in the first place. There are dozens of things you can do to take yourself out of the high-rick category for heart problems. They are:

Stop Smoking

Is there really any need to tell you this? You smoke — you die, that is, you die a lot sooner. You might say: everyone has to die from something sooner or later. That's true. You have to die, but you don't have to die from smoking. Death doesn't give us a choice about the way we go when it comes eventually, but you can have some choice right now in your life — stop smoking.

After you quit, your chances of suffering from heart disease start to subside immediately. It's true that it takes 10 years to get back to the risk of a total nonsmoker, but even after the first year your risk drops to half! And just 30 days after you quit smoking, your beneficial cholesterol levels rise and your bad cholesterol goes down.

Speaking of cholesterol

One of the primary causes of heart attacks is chunks of hardened grease and fat — cholesterol — clogging up the arteries which serve your heart. When a passage gets totally blocked, your heart is in a heap of trouble.

Turn to the "Cholesterol" section in this book for tons of easy and effective ways to reduce your cholesterol level.

By the way, if you want to know what "safe" cholesterol levels are, here are the risk levels based on age, according to the National Heart, Lung and Blood Institute:

Age	Moderate Risk	High Risk
2-19	Greater than 170	Greater than 185
20-29	Greater than 200	Greater than 220
30-39	Greater than 220	Greater than 240

Above 40   Greater than 240   Greater than 260

Get a cholesterol test to find out what your level is, then go to work at bringing it down point-by-point. Make a game of it! See how effective you can be. Challenge someone else to a contest. See who can top 50 points the fastest. It'll be great fun, and you'll find yourself feeling better and better along the way.

Eskimos never have heart attacks

It's true.   Studies of Native Alaskans found that heart disease was nearly nonexistent among the ice dwellers. Scientists believe it's the high amount of fish in their diet, and specifically, the high levels of a fish oil called omega-3. You can buy omega-3 supplements, but using these is less effective than eating the fish themselves. Also, taking fish oil capsules can have negative side effects, including digestive upset, bloating, burping, even dizziness. It's best to eat a lot of baked mackerel, canned tuna and salmon, (and skip frying it in butter!)

Regular meditators have less heart attacks

Heart attacks are not all physiologically generated. Your state of mind contributes greatly to your heart rate, blood pressure, breathing, and many other factors which affect your heart directly.

Studies show that people who meditate just 10 minutes per day have more than 60 percent fewer heart attack than people who do nothing to deal with their daily stress.

See the "Meditation" section is this book for an easy method of meditation that anyone can learn immediately. Just 10 minutes a day could save your life.

Lose weight

The more weight you carry on your body the harder your heart must to work to keep all portions of your body supplied with blood and oxygen. The link between obesity and heart disease is no longer a mere link — it's a full-blown, eight-lane bridge. Carrying extra weight on your body is extra strain on your heart. For every pound you lose, your risk of heart attack goes down incrementally. The "obesity" section in this book contains an excellent 35-point plan to help you shed the pounds.

What about brandy?

You may have heard that a shot of brandy per day is good for the heart. Is it? It may be in some cases. All alcohol has the effect of relaxing the muscles and dilating the arteries in the heart. Drinking brandy has also been shown to increase the amount of "good cholesterol" in your blood as opposed to the "bad cholesterol."

But although drinking a bit of brandy every day is not likely to hurt, don't expect it to do the total job — that is, provide you with complete protection against heart attack and heart disease. A drink a day of brandy, or any other alcoholic beverage, quickly becomes addictive and leads to even more drinking, and then you've got an increase in health problems, not a decrease. Remember that alcohol is basically a poison to your body in any amount. The negative effects of a drink a day could easily outweigh the benefits it could have for your heart.

An aspirin a day

The evidence is conclusive now that taking one aspirin a day has tremendous benefits in reducing heart attack risk. Aspirin does this by rendering the blood less capable of clotting. Some people don't handle aspirins well, however.

If you are asthmatic, you should avoid aspirin. If you have stomach problems, especially an ulcer, you obviously won't be able to handle aspirin. Don't think that other drugs, such as Tylenol, will provide the same heart health benefits as aspirin. Tylenol contains an entirely different drug than aspirin and it won't have the same effect.

What about coffee?

It's best to avoid more than a cup a day if you are a high-risk heart person. You all know the way caffeine can make your heart flutter, although some other aspects of caffeine may actually benefit your heart. The net result is, though, a negative one from coffee. Drinking a lot of coffee also makes it much more difficult to reduce your cholesterol level. Certain oils and other chemicals in coffee, for unknown reasons, cause many people to have sky-rocketing cholesterol levels, which is the worse possible thing for your heart.

What about sex?

Well, what about it? Will having sex with a bad heart increase your chances of having a heart attack, Like any strenuous exercise. Before you do something to take yourself out of the high-risk category for heart attacks, you never know what may trigger an attack. The best evidence seems to suggest, however, that the risk of a heart attack during sex is actually very small. In a study of 5,000 men who had already suffered a heart attack, less than 20 died from heart attacks during sex after being released from the hospital. Those are pretty good odds.

Exercise

This is another of those "do we even have to tell you about it?" category. Your heart is a muscle, and like any muscle, it responds by becoming stronger if exercised properly. Of course, if you are already overweight and have heart problems, you'll need to avoid strenuous exercise. For a person with heart problems, even a calm stroll through a park can bring on heart palpitations, shortness of breath and possible heart attack. But see your doctor for an exercise program that can whip your heart into shape a little at a time.

You must avoid salt

That salty taste you love so much on french fries and potato chips has little love for your heart. To put it simply, salt causes your blood vessels to restrict, making it harder for your heart to pump blood through them. The harder the heart has to work, the higher your blood pressure gets, and the more likely you are to have a heart attack, stroke or some other problem.

What about your attitude?

The way you live your life, and your general outlook on the world and towards other people has a much bigger influence on your heart health than you might imagine.

Although most people no longer associate the heart with emotions and cognitive aspects of life, the ancients were at least intuitively correct when they considered the heart the center of the soul.

If you maintain a generally negative, pessimistic, blaming, jealous, angry attitude, it can really lead to serious heart disease. Another great source of heart disease is fear. Fear can be a part of your life subtly, or an obvious problem. If you live in a high-crime neighborhood, if you have a dangerous job, if a member or your household is frequently threatening or violent, this persistent climate of fear will wreak havoc on your heart.

Psychologists studying the physiological effects of fear in the laboratory found that rats which were subjected to constant fear situations developed heart problems and other organ diseases at rates as much as a thousand times greater than rats who lead peaceful, happy lives.

One group of rats, for example, were put in pails of water and allowed to thrash around until they nearly drowned. After being taken out to rest for a while, it was back in the pail again. After just a week or so of this, the rats were killed and dissected for examination of their internal organs.

As it turns out, the heart tissue of these poor creatures had aged far in advance of other rats of the same age. The conclusion was obvious — constant fear and stress hardened and dried out the hearts of those stressed out rats. Fear, stress, anger and other such emotions have the same effect on your heart.

If you live in a dangerous neighborhood, move if you can. If you have an attitude of anger and resentment, it's time to take a serious look into your soul and see what you can do to change it. That could be any one of a million things, but ultimately it's up to you to examine your life and see what can be done to bring some joy, happiness, love and forgiveness into it.

Love truly is one of the best medicines for the heart. That's a scientific fact! Seek it out, and live a longer, healthier, happier life.

Heart Palpitations

Just what are they? A heart palpitation is an extra beat of the heart — sort of beat in between beats. It's a frightening thing when it happens to you — as is any strange feeling in your heart.

Palpitations are described as "flutters or a feeling that the heart has "jumped."

Palpitations can be brought on by too much coffee, any kind of amphetamine, smoking or stress and anxiety. They can also result from sudden movement, such as getting out of bed too quickly or jumping up to catch the telephone.

What to do about palpitations

A heart palpitation is most often nothing to worry about if it happens a great once and a while. It's simply your body trying to catch up to you — or, more likely, it is your body sending you a strong message that it has had enough poison for the day.

Maybe you should think twice about that tenth cup of coffee, or decide not to tear open the seal on that third pack of cigarettes of the day. Are you taking too many diet pills, or stressing yourself out all day without a rest? Are you eating properly, and we're not talking about an order of McNuggets and a diet Coke.

The good thing about heart palpitations is that they are almost entirely within your control. What you need to do is avoid the offending substances that are causing the problem. If your heart is fluttering, then you truly need to wean yourself from the coffee and cigarettes. If you are taking drugs, legal or illegal, you better see your doctor or knock it off. If you have a high stress job, ask yourself if your job is worth dying for. If you absolutely can't quit your job, then you need to do things that will help you drain away the stress of it all. How about 10 minutes a day of meditation? How about taking a break now and then to simply breath? How about finding a nice quite place for a time out or a 15-minute cat nap?

On the other hand, if your heart palpitations are frequent

and persistent, you may need a prescription drug to regulate your heart rate. In that case, you may have a more serious condition, but even in that case, taking the precautions described above will only help your situation.

The Heart Murmur

This occurs when a heart valve is defective in some way. The turbulence of blood moving through a bad valve is what causes the murmur. Causes are rheumatic fever, high blood pressure, heart enlargements and hearts that have grown defectively from birth.

A heart murmur can be completely harmless, or it can be the source of a serious medical problem. Usually, you need a doctor to identify a heart murmur by listening to your heart with a stethoscope. He or she will tell you how bad it is and whether you need further treatment or not. In the meantime, you can help your heart along with the proper diet, by avoiding pollutants like tobacco, coffee and alcohol, and with exercise that does not aggravate your murmur further.

Other heart diseases

There are many kinds of heart disease — from enlargening of the heart, to viral infections and parasites which attack this vital organ of your body. Sometimes heart problems are the result of birth defects, or outside influences, but most of the time, they are the result of how you are living your life.

The vast majority of us are born with a heart that is in A-1 condition. All we have to do is treat it properly, and it will carry us through a long life, beating away and pumping blood, supplying oxygen and vital nutrients to the rest of your body.

If you treat it properly, it won't fail you. It's a real tragedy that more than a half-million Americans die every year through self abuse. It doesn't have to be that way. Eat right, live right, be kind, forgiving and happy, and your heart will always be a source of life affirming joy for you and the people around you.

Heartburn

You may be one of 80 or 100 million people in the U.S. who never stray too far from a pack of Rolaids because it seems that just about anything you eat sets your chest afire with heartburn.

Heartburn has little or nothing to do with your heart. The problem is with the door between your esophagus and stomach. As you know, your stomach contains powerful acids used to digest foods. When the doorway to the stomach — called the esophageal sphincter — fails to close properly, it lets acid from the stomach back up into your esophagus. While your stomach is designed for digestive acids, your esophagus is not, and the result is a powerful burning sensation.

So how do you get the doorway to close properly? Well, don't do things that will weaken the esophageal sphincter, and those things are:

(a) Smoking. Once again, the Demon Weed finds a new way to create trouble in your life. Smoking cigarettes weakens the esophageal sphincter considerably. Don't complain about heartburn if you're not trying to curb your smoking. Without stopping, you don't have much chance of booting the problem.

(b) No napping. It seems almost natural to take a nap after a big meal, but that makes gravity work against you. Acid will more easily travel upward into your esophagus if your are horizontal. Let your food digest a bit before you lie down.

(c) No bedtime snacks. Your stomach can produce acid for up to seven hours after you eat. If you eat just before you go to bed, you may be setting yourself up for a late-night acid or heartburn attack that will ruin your sleep, and thus the following day. Skip the bedtime snack if you are prone to heartburn.

(c) Avoid Stress. Perhaps the No. 1 cause of heartburn behind coffee and cigarettes is stress and anxiety. Stress, fear and anxiety gets the acid factory in your stomach pumping. Take time out, or a meditation break to calm yourself and your body down. (See headings under "Meditation", "Stress").

(d) Coffee, chocolate and caffeine. Avoid them all. Make no doubt about it — they are all major, we repeat MAJOR, causes of heartburn. (See heading under "Three Terrible C's").

What will help

(a) Milk, antacids, bicarbonate of soda or soda crackers. All of these are well known counter-agents of heartburn and they usually work, so why not try them?

(b) Lose weight. A common contributor to heartburn is obesity. Losing weight will be good for your total health, so do it for more than easing heartburn.

(c) Eat smaller meals more often. Rather than big honking meals that distend your belly and make you waddle like a duck, easing food into your stomach a little at a time all day will give your stomach a chance to digest, and will not force food upwards to make room in limited space.

Persistent heartburn

Many TV commercials now warn about the dangers of persistent heartburn, while at the same time pushing their over-the-counter products as the solution. This makes little sense. If you have long-term, recurring heartburn, and if you need to keep taking over-the-counter medicine day after day, then you probably should see a doctor. Remember, frequent heartburn can lead to more serious problems, such as ulcers, gastritis (inflammation of the stomach wall), stomach cancer and other problems. Use your common sense. Deal with it.

Hemorrhoids

Selling products to fight hemorrhoids, also known as piles, is a major industry in the United States. People spend millions and billions every year for relief of this painful, embarrassing problem which makes something as simple as sitting through a movie a painful ordeal.

Hemorrhoids are varicose veins of the rectum that bulge out, push on the skin and nerve endings, and cause incredible pain. Hemorrhoids can be outside the sphincter or actually inside the anal passage. Hemorrhoids can crack the skin causing anal fissures, which bleed and burn.

And it can get even worse. A blood clot in a hemorrhoid, called a thrombosed hemorrhoid, can grow to the size of a grape. Any physical contact, like a tissue wipe, against that horrid little grape means pain beyond pain.

Preventing Piles

As we discussed in the section about anal fissures, stool that is hard and difficult to pass is a major cause and irritant of hemorrhoids. The main cause of hard stool is a low-fiber diet full of fats and sugar.

So do yourself a favor — soften up your stools with some decent high-fiber food. That means lots more vegetables and lots less meat and breads — unless the bread is whole grain. Eat more beans, rice, corn, wheat bran, bulgar, apples, bananas and other fruits and vegetables. Your stool will soften and going to the bathroom will not be a source of major pain. It will also give your hemorrhoids a chance to heal.

If you have a sitting job

If you are a truck driver or desk worker, sitting for eight hours at a time puts tremendous pressure on the veins in your rectal area. Sitting for long periods without a break is just asking for trouble with hemorroids. Always take a break and get up every hour, or at least every two hours. If you are a truck driver, get out of that truck once a while, rather than bouncing around on your bum for 10 hours while you drive yourself to hemorrhoid hell.

Do the exercise

An exercise that strengthens your rectal muscles involves squeezing them hard, as one does after a bowel movement. Do it for 30 seconds each time for several times while walking around for about 15 minutes. Adding this routine to break up your daily sitting schedule will prevent piles.

Keep it clean

Sometimes the worst part of hemorrhoids is the burning, itching and irritation. That can be resolved by a cleaner rectum. Take more baths. Perhaps a spray wash is called for after each bowel movement rather than just wiping. Go the extra mile if you have to. And don't rub yourself too hard. Be gentle with that toilet paper, and use only white toilet paper. The dyes in colored or scented toilet paper can cause further irritation or start future hemorrhoids.

Long baths

This is nothing new to you, but sometimes the oldest advice is still the best. Long baths with Epsom salts will soothe your hemorrhoids, reduce swelling and itching, and just ease your pile problem.

Preparation ??

Should you use over-the-counter hemorrhoid medications? You probably don't need us to tell you the answer to that. If you have hemorrhoids, you've likely already tried many of them, and you have probably found they help quite a bit, right? If they don't, and you feel you have a major pain and a major problem, perhaps more serious medicine is needed, in which case you'll need a doctor.

Other Rectal Pain

Don't assume that all rectal pain is caused by hemorrhoids. Other possibilities are an ulceration, a rectal polyp, rectal cancer, or anal fissures, which are basically tears or cracks in the skin. Any of these will make bowel movements a painful experience.

See the heading under "Anal fissures" and "Colon problems" for more information on how to help or deal with all of these complications. And remember, starting on a high-fiber, low-fat diet as soon as possible will go a long way toward helping any condition which affects the rectum or lower colon.

Hiatal Hernia

We talk about heartburn in another section of this book, and the primary symptom of a hiatal hernia is just that — heartburn.

But this illness deserves its own category because the cause is different from ordinary heartburn, which for the most part is just acid that backs up from your stomach into the esophagus.

A hiatal hernia involves a small part of the stomach itself slipping up into your esophagus and taking acid with it. In addition to heartburn, there can be added pain and belching.

A hiatal hernia is different from the more common inguinal hernia, which involves a portion of the small intestine breaking through a weak spot in the abdominal wall. This usually happens after heavy lifting, coughing or accidents. To deal with these, you need a doctor to push the intestine back to where it belongs, although many people live with such a hernia for a long while.

But if you have a hiatal hernia, there is much you can do about it on your own. Try the following:

Putting pressure on it

Like in heartburn, you want to do everything you can to

make the esophageal sphincter close more tightly. You want to reduce the pressure coming up from the stomach. The following substances will not help you in that department:

Alcohol
Coffee, tea and any caffeine source
Chocolate
Greasy, high fat foods
Peppermint or spearmint
Tobacco products

Taking pressure off of it

Anything you do to squeeze in on your stomach will force pressure upward — exactly what you don't want to do. Try wearing suspenders instead of a belt that may be too tight. Don't bend over on a full stomach. Don't lie down for a nap because that makes gravity work against you. You don't want to help your food go uphill when you want it to stay downhill.

Lose weight

As it helps with heartburn, losing weight will be a major help with a hiatal hernia.

Go the veggie route

Statistical studies show that vegetarians have less incidence of hiatal hernia than meat eaters. The reason a vegetarian diet is better is,it is lower in fat and has more fiber. Fatty, greasy foods, especially meats, are terrible for a person prone to digestive problems, such as hernias, gastritis, irritable colon, heartburn, stomach ulcers and other problems. Of course, fat and grease do nothing to take off weight, and staying heavy only means a hernia that gets worse.

One note of contradiction, however: certain lean meats such as white turkey and white chicken without the skin can help build the strength of your esophageal sphincter muscle. Adding a bit of those to your high-vegetable diet will ease your cravings for meat and help you with your hernia at the same time.

Diets high in fiber are especially beneficial for hernia problems. High-fiber diets aid digestion in a number of ways, and also prevent or lessen all kinds of problems, from anal fissures to diabetes. More beans, rice, wheat bran and all kinds of vegetables will help you out a lot.

"Hidden" Toxics In Your Life

Is your Carpet a Hazard To Your Health?

You likely have heard of lead poisoning, mostly from traces of lead in the water supply and lead content in old paint chips.

But a source of unhealthy lead may be lurking right under your feet.   Carpeting, especially the plush, shag-pile variety, may contain lead amounts which exceed federal safety standards.

A recent study of the dust vacuumed from rugs in 37 different homes found that among all the dirt, dust and gunk were considerable concentrations of lead. Toddlers who crawl and play on the rugs inevitably put their hands in their mouths and ingest lead dust.

Scientist think lead gets into carpets from the bottoms of

shoes. People who walk frequently near streets alongside heavy traffic can pick up the traces of lead from automobile emissions. The soil around houses can be contaminated with lead from years of painting, scraping and re-painting of houses with paints that used to contain lead. Although lead has been eliminated from paint and gasoline for more than a decade, the build-up which occurred over many years has left some areas permanently contaminated.

The best way to avoid lead build-up in your carpet is to have strict rules in your house against walking on the carpet with shoes. Of course, you could always get rid of your carpeting all together, or at least switch to flat rugs, which will absorb less lead.

In addition to lead, other kinds of toxics can travel from your shoes to your carpet, such as pesticides and herbicides on your lawn, or chemicals used on streets, which may contain harmful benzene and other substances.

Aluminum everywhere

Small amounts of the shiny metal aluminum which finds its way into our food and water, and then into your body, may be causing a multitude of health problems in your life.

Aluminum poisoning has been connected to iron-deficiency anemia, , brain damage, migraine headaches, cancer, bone thinning, intestinal disorders and Alzheimer's Disease. Some researchers believe that as many as one in three people have their health affected by aluminum.

Studies of patients with Alzheimer's consistently show tiny deposits of aluminum at the center of certain lesions on the brain, which are believed by some researchers to cause Alzheimer's.

Aluminum has penetrated our lives in an amazing number

of ways. Perhaps the most significant is aluminum cookware. Aluminum cookware dissolves in food. If yourcheck your own aluminum pans, you may notice pitting or tiny areas where the metal has been removed. Many of the acids and alkalies in food dissolve aluminum, as do cleansers and hard water.

You would do yourself a favor if you got rid of all your aluminum cookware and replaced it with stainless steel, enamel, Pyrex, cast-iron or eathenware.

But there are also many other sources of aluminum in your daily life. Many municipal water companies use an aluminum-containing chemical to treat water that can build up in your body over time and cause Alzheimer's or other health problems.

Here are some other possible sources of aluminum:

cake mixes	salad dressing
pickles	baking powder
table salt	grated or powdered cheeses
cosmetics	anti-perspirants
pop cans	some brands of aspirin

Not that not all cake mixes or aspirin brands or other products contain aluminum, but you should check labels carefully, or even write to product manufacturers to enquire about possible aluminum content in their products.

Remember also that most restaurants use aluminum cookware, so if you really want to go all the way to avoid aluminum in your diet, avoid eating out often.

Hypoglycemia

This may or may not be a condition within itself. Hypoglycemia is closely associated with diabetes, another disease which involves deficient levels of sugar within your blood stream.

Hypoglycemia is simply having too little sugar in the blood. The symptoms can be dizziness; fainting; cold, clammy skin; and breaking out in a sweat.

Since these symptoms are brought on by too little sugar in the blood, a quick fix is to replenish it. Drink some orange juice or some other fruit juice with a high glucose content to bring your condition under control.

But the real solution to hypoglycemia is to eat foods that contain complex, long-chin carbohydrates that provide your blood with a steady level of glucose over long periods of time. Pasta, whole grains, potatoes and other such foods will keep you in balance.

While hypoglycemia involves too little sugar in the blood, eating sweets is not a very good idea for people with this condition. The reason is that, whenever you dump sugar into your system, your body reacts by injecting more insulin into your bloodstream to take care of it. Increased insulin is associated with that sluggish and depressive feeling that many people associate with sugar bingeing. For people with hypoglycemia, the reaction can be worse than just a little sluggishness.

You should not skip meals if you have hypoglycemia. Skipping meals only makes low blood sugar worse.

Hypoglycemia is usually nothing to worry about if you remember to watch your diet, make sure you don't skip meals and watch your intake of sweets.

Indigestion

If you have plain old indigestion, then you don't have a very serious problem. Indigestion is simply the sick feeling you get when your stomach is upset by something you dumped into it. Too much food, too much alcohol, too much smoking, or foods that are too spicy or different from your usual diet.

Ordinary indigestion happens to just about everyone once in a while and if you have an ounce of common sense, then you have more than an ounce of prevention.

The number one cure? Wait. That's it — just wait. Why deny it? Sometimes all kinds of fancy methodologies and clever folk remedies are no more helpful than waiting patiently for your rumbling to pass. Just know that it will, endure it for now and realize that "all things pass."

If you are experiencing an upset stomach while eating, you should stop and give your stomach a rest. The fix can be as simple as that. Don't stuff yourself during your meals, and lose some extra pounds if you can. By now, you should know what foods set you off — avoid them. If you absolutely love Cajun shrimp or curried chicken and you want to eat it anyway — be prepared to pay the consequences. Don't worry, it won't last. If it does, try an ordinary antacid — that's what they're for.

You may also try drinking something that will make you burp — any carbonated beverage will do. Also, an excellent stomach settler is peppermint tea. Sip on a cup while you sit back and relax — but don't lie down. That may cause your stomach acid to come upward causing heartburn on top of your unsettled stomach!

Will milk make it better?

In fact, milk may make your indigestion worse because it can raise the level of acid in your stomach. On the other hand, many people swear by the soothing effect of milk. Really, this is a low-risk experiment if you want to try some milk on your upset stomach. Find out for yourself. Other drinks, though, like coffee and tea will most likely make you worse. Coffee and caffeine really jack up the acid levels in your stomach. If you are prone to stomach upset, drinking coffee and smoking are flirting with disaster.

When indigestion is something worse

Of course, your indigestion could be telling you that you have a much more serious problem, like gastritis (inflammation of the inner stomach) an ulcer, stomach cancer, colon problem or others. The key is persistence of your upset stomach. Everyone gets a little stomach ache now and then. But if you have one a lot, then it's time to look more deeply into the problem.

Remember a low-fat, high-fiber diet

You probably don't need a book to tell you that a diet high in easy-to-digest fruits and vegetables, and high in fiber will result in less indigestion and a more stable stomach in general. Make fruits and vegetables the major part of your meal, while meats become the side dish. You'll see. Your stomach upset will become virtually nonexistent.

Kidney Stones

What is tiny as a grain of sand, but strong enough to put a 300-pound football player down on the turf? Well, a kidney stone could do it.

Kidney stones are not usually as big as stones. They tend to be tiny, like seeds, but they can get as big as a golf ball. But even a tiny grain in your kidney can be extremely painful. A stone can also produce vomiting, fever, chills, blood in the urine, irritable bladder and bloating.

If you have a pain in the small of your back which moves around to the front and possibly shoots into the groin, then you very likely have a kidney stone.

Kidney stones are most often made up of calcium which absorbs and collects in your kidneys if they are not flushed with enough liquids, or if you happen to have a body that has a high calcium absorption rate.

Drink that water

The best way to make sure that you never get a painful kidney stone is to drink a lot of water every day. If you are a coffee drinker or a soda-holic, you will be better off switching to plain old water. It's a lot more boring, but it will keep you out of trouble. And once you get used to it, water can be as much of an oral gratification as any other drink can be.

Avoid these foods

Specifically, the substance of most kidney stones is something called calcium oxalate. You are probably already familiar with foods that are high in calcium, such as dairy products, but there is another group of foods high in oxalates. While most of these foods are extremely healthy for most people, those of you who are prone to kidney stones should avoid them. Here they are:

Asparagus	Almonds
blackberries	chocolate
beets	chard
green beans	cranberries
currants	figs
oranges	plums
strawberries	rhubarb
raspberries	lamb
okra	spinach
tomato	sweet potato
pepper	poppy seed

Again, all of these foods are mostly excellent nutritional foods that can prevent cancer and heart disease. But if you have a great deal of certainty about your chances of developing a kidney stone, the above are no-nos.

Vitamin C

For once, we are not going to recommend vitamin C as a remedy for a physical illness. It seems like vitamin C is good for just about any condition you can have, but when it comes to kidney stones, too much C is not recommended because it helps your body absorb calcium. Now that's great if you have high blood pressure or osteoarthritis, but not if you have a kidney stone. You can still eat foods rich in vitamin C, but vitamin C tablets are not the way to go.

Vitamin D, too

Vitamin D also helps absorption of calcium, so getting too much of this is not good either. Here are some foods high in Vitamin D:

Salmon	mackerel
sardines	tuna
dry cereals	milk

Eat a lot of broccoli and rice

Studies show that broccoli contains a lot of enzymes that reduce the chances of kidney stones being formed. Broccoli is the number one cancer-fighting vegetable. It is also one of the best for kidney and urinary tract health. Broccoli clearly is a "super food" that few of us can afford to restrict from our diet.

Studies also show that diets high in rice go a long way toward limiting kidney problems. Eating more rice and rice bran along with your broccoli will do your kidneys good.

Avoid salt

More salt can lead to more kidney stones — it's as simple as that. There are lots of reasons to restrict salt from your diet, so there's one more.

Do all of the above and ...

Drink tons of water, eat the right foods and avoid the wrong foods and your kidney stone may disappear on its own over time. If it doesn't, your only other option may be surgery or ultrasound therapy.

If you have already had a painful kidney stone attack, there is a 100 percent chance that you will have one again unless you deal with it in some way. Of the one million attacks experienced by Americans each year, about a third are severe enough to require admission to a hospital, and most likely will require a major-league pain killer, like morphine or some other narcotic.

If you suspect you have a major kidney stone, get it checked out. Stones can also be caused by other physical problems, such as thyroid problems or other hormonal imbalances.

Meditation for Health

There are perhaps as many ways to meditate as there are people who practice this mental and physical discipline, which bestows almost unlimited health benefits on those who use it regularly.

Since this is a book of tips on how to improve your health, we'll look at some simple meditation techniques you can practice for just 5 to 10 minutes per day that will yield tremendous benefits to your mental and physical well-being.

First, a couple facts about meditation that may make you feel more comfortable with it.

Meditation is not necessarily a religious exercise. It is not associated exclusively with eastern religions, such as Zen and Buddhism, the Sufi sects of Islam, the Yogi masters of India, or others. Meditation is not something only people involved in cults or esoteric eastern religions do. There are many forms of Christian meditation as well. Meditation techniques have nothing to do with religion what-so-ever.

Just because you decide to practice meditation does not mean you have to abandon your current religion, nor does it mean you are doing anything that is "weird" or somehow philosophically unwholesome.

Meditation is safe for anyone to practice. Meditation does not involve going into a trance, or putting yourself in a state of mind that will make you passive, or open to unwanted mental intrusions from negative sources.

Meditation also does not involve sitting in an uncomfortable, contorted position on the floor, burning incense or chanting — unless you choose to do those things.

Simply put, meditation merely involves sitting quietly, clearing your mind of troubles and turmoil, and seeking a feeling of peace and centeredness.

How to meditate

So now that we have done away with some of the myths of meditation, let's try it out.

Meditation can be incredibly simple, yet deceptively difficult at times. The whole trick of meditation (if there is a trick at all) is to sit or lie down quietly and release everything from your mind, whether it be positive or negative thoughts.

Try this:

Find a chair in a quiet room where there are no other people, no television or radio playing, and no other distractions.

Sit in your chair, but don't sit like you usually do. Sit closer to the edge of the chair. Put your feet flat on the floor, and keep your back straight. Put your hands palms down on your knees. You should be able to draw a straight line from the bottom of your spine, up through your back, neck and the back of your head — and the line would be perpendicular with the ceiling.

Don't try to be too stiff, as if a metal rod has been rammed down your spine. Just keep yourself generally straight, as if you were trying to practice good posture.

The next thing you want to do is take three slow, deep breaths. As you inhale imagine that you are drawing positive energy into your body, and as you exhale, imagine that all pain and negativity is rushing out of your body. Do it anyway you want. Some people like to imagine a stream of golden, positive energy entering their body as they inhale, and black or gray negative energy leaving their body as they exhale. But it's really up to you how you want to visualize this. It's usually best to invent your own way.

After doing three big breaths, you will probably notice that your mind is more quiet and more focused, that your heart rate is more steady, and you are feeling more calm.

The next thing you want to do is to simply see how long you can maintain this peaceful mental state, concentrating on your breathing, and keeping your mental activity to a minimum. The first day, try for 5 minutes and eventually work your way up to 10 minutes per session.

An important tip: Don't try too hard to keep your mind clear and calm. The harder you try, the more difficult you will find it to keep your mind empty.

You will find that all kinds of thoughts will persistently intrude on your attempt to remain calm and empty. It's incredibly difficult to let go of the million things we all have to think about each day — but that's the whole purpose of meditation — to give yourself a break from the daily chatter in your mind.

Don't worry, it's only for ten minutes. You can go back to whatever thoughts or worries you wish after your meditation session has been completed. But for just this ten minutes, once per day, commit yourself to a calm mind.

And at this point you might be thinking: How could anything so simple and uncomplicated really do me any good, especially for only 5 to 10 minutes per day?

But the facts are — and there is an enormous amount of medical data to back this up — that meditation can do everything from lower your blood pressure, to cure cancer, heal your heart, lower your cholesterol level, ease your addictions and much more.

Meditation is widely regarded by those inside and outside the medical community as one of the most powerful tools available for both preventative health care, and for easing existing conditions.

Because most of our lives are so fast-paced, and so filled with endless stress and activities, the precious ten minutes you give yourself once a day may be the very oasis of sanity that will allow your body to catch up and strengthen itself against the daily onslaught of the fast-paced American lifestyle, which most of us face everyday.

To sum up:

To meditate you need to remember only four basic things:

(1) Find a quite, undisturbed place where you can be alone for 10 minutes without distractions.

(2) Sit in a comfortable, upright posture, with back straight and face forward, hands on your knees. You may also lie flat on your back with hands at your sides or on your stomach.

(3) Concentrate on your breathing while ignoring all your other thoughts. Note: it is extremely important that you

don't try to "fight off" your thoughts. This will only make them louder and more persistent. Just let them run past you — let your mind flow like a stream, a stream which you pay little attention to.

(4) Do it at least once a day, although a ten minute session in the morning and an equal one at night will bring optimum results.

You've done it!

That's all there is to it! If you practice this simple meditation once or twice a day, you may start noticing results in your daily life and general level of health immediately. If you don't get immediate results, stick with it for two weeks. If by then you can still say meditation has done you no good, then you've wasted little time, and you'll know this stuff is not for you.

Mental Health Report

Are counselor's and psychologists a waste of time and money?

We have come to live in a time some people are calling the "Therapy Culture." An explosion of self-help groups have mushroomed throughout America. Everything from Yeast Infections Anonymous (no kidding) to Emotions Anonymous have sprung up, all based loosely on the grandfather of self help groups, Alcoholics Anonymous.

In addition to self-help groups, people seeking the help of a psychiatrist, psychologist or some other type of councelor have made mental illness or emotional problems, even minor emotional problems, a major growth industry.

But do self-help groups and counselors really do any good? Can they do more harm than good? Some people are beginning to question the assumptions we have come to hold about mental health care, and many are taking a second look at the now commonly held assumption that "everyone is disfunctional."

To Feel or Not to Feel — That is the Question

A lot of people put off living their lives to the fullest as they seek counseling to become less depressed, to cope with their fears, to reduce their anxiety, and so on. The therapy culture tells people that they are "out of touch with their feelings." It says that until people search deeply within themselves for a thorough self examination of their feelings, they won't be able to achieve success or happiness.

Now psychologists, such as James Hillman and David Reynolds, say that all this interest in individual "feelings" may be a bunch of hogwash. They ask you to consider this:

• Sometimes if we aren't aware of our feelings, that doesn't mean we have lost touch with ourselves. Rather, it may be that we just aren't feeling anything — period.

• We are the experts on our own feelings, not some counselor or psychiatrist.

• Feelings don't always have to be expressed or "released" as long as they are acknowledged.

• Many feelings are complex and cannot be adequately described — that doesn't mean you are confused or out of touch.

• Feelings don't need to be fixed. All you have to do is feel them — that's it.

• Feelings need not hinder us from getting on with life and doing what we need to do.

• Being happy or comfortable or anxiety free all the time may not only be impossible, but it may not be all that important.

• As long as feeling good is the top priority of our culture, we can expect problems with drugs, psychotherapy, crime and other social problems.
I'll achieve great things — when my problems have been solved

Hillman and Reynolds say millions of people are moping around, spending thousands of dollars on psychologists and generally feeling sorry for themselves when they should be getting on with life and getting things done.

If you wait for that day when you are feeling totally happy and free, then you will have a long wait, because until you get off your butt and accomplish something, you'll never be happy.

In fact, relying on counseling and psychotherapy may be blocking you from your goals in life and your success because it has led you to believe that someday — some far day in the future — you will feel a lot better about yourself, and that's when you'll get what you want in life.

The moral of the story is: If you're feeling bad or depressed or stressed or anxiety — that may be just what you need right now. What's certain is that all things pass. If you simply press forward and strive toward your goals, you may find that your subsequent accomplishments will deliver to you the life you have always wanted, and feelings of happiness.

And ... no matter how much money you pay your therapist ... he/she will never deliver you happiness on a silver platter. Never ever.

Menstrual Problems and PMS

Menstrual Cramps

They're "all in your head," right? That's been the long-held belief about menstrual cramps, especially in pre-feminist movement days, when just about anything a woman thought, talked about or believed in was considered to be a lot of airy-fairy nonsense.

No longer. The truth is, menstrual cramps are real and are not in the head, but in the cervix.

Some women produce clots of blood while they menstruate. These clots cause pain when they try to move through the cervix, which is the opening from the uterus to the vagina. The problem can get worse if endometriosis develops. Endometriosis is a disease that involves cells — which ordinarily line the wall of the uterus — getting into places they do not belong, such as the bladder, intestinal wall or other places outside the uterus. Another disease that can make menstruation painful is pelvic inflammatory disease.

Yet another cause of menstrual cramps is a chemical called prostaglandins, which cause the uterine muscles to contract and expel tissue and fluids during menstruation. When the levels of prostaglandins gets too high, the result is more cramping than is necessary to complete the job of menstruation.

Anti-cramping exercises

Here are three excellent exercises that will be beneficial in relieving menstrual cramps and aiding blood flow.

The Fish

(1) If you can, sit in a lotus position or cross-legged on the floor, "Indian style."

(2) Now you want to bend backwards. Lower yourself down on your elbows until the back of your head is on the floor.

(3) Continue to press down on your elbows and move your hands down under your thighs.

(4) Now exhale as you increase the arch of your back as much as possible, holding onto your legs if necessary.

(5) Now lift your outstretched arms over your head and rest them on the floor.

(6) Hold this position for 10 seconds to a minute, or as long as you can.

(7) Breath normally and relax. Repeat.

Leg Spreads

(1) Stand with your feet as wide apart as possible.

(2) With hands on the waists, bend forward while exhaling, keeping your back arched backwards.

(3) When your upper body is parallel to the floor, bring the hands down to the floor, and place your palms down flat, with your fingers pointing forward.

(4) Inhale and lift up your head.

(5) Exhale, and lower the top of your head to the floor.

(6) Hold position for as long as you can, but no longer than a minute. Relax. Breath. Do it again.

The Reclining Warrior

(1) Kneel in an upright position, knees together with your feet about a foot-and-a-half apart.

(2) Lower yourself down and sit between your knees and legs on the floor.

(3) Now you want to lean backwards, using your hands or elbows to help yourself on the way down, and you want to end up on your back with your knees and legs still bent beneath you.

(4) When you are resting on the back of your head, shoulders and back, bring your arms up over your head and lay them on the floor. elbows straight.

(5) You can hold this pose for as long as ten minutes as your body stretches out and relaxes.

Doing these and other Yoga-style stretching exercises can free and loosen your body, and greatly aid in easier, cramp-free menstrual cycles. Of course, losing weight and keeping up a regular exercise schedule will make you more healthy in all aspects of your life, including relieving physical and mental stress which aids in menstruation.

Some other anti-cramping advice

Unclotting

It stands to reason that if your blood is clotting and causing cramps, you should do something to thin the blood. Good old common aspirin is what accomplishes that. Aspirins will not only relieve pain, but help your blood flow more freely without clotting. Not only is aspirin good, but other over-the-counter drugs which contain the active ingredient, ibuprofin, is very effective against menstrual cramps because it inhibits the production of prostaglandins. Advil, Nuprin and other common pills contain ibuprofin.

Lose the fat in your diet

Having a high fat, high cholesterol diet leads to more menstrual cramping. Go to a high-fiber, vegetable-dominant diet. While it might not help right away with the cramps you are having right now, by the time next month's period comes around, you could have a much easier time of it.

Sexual Activity

A long-time myth still held by many people is that you should never have sex during a period, but there's really no basis for it beyond psychological factors. If you don't mind the messiness, there's nothing wrong with sex during a period and, in fact, the exercise will help menstrual flow.

Warmth helps, but cold doesn't hurt

Many people believe that cold, rainy weather makes cramping and a period worse, but this is untrue. Getting chilled will not stop the blood flow, although just the opposite may make the blood flow better. Applying warmth to your stomach will loosen things up for you, ease the flow and cramping.

Coffee, alcohol and other diuretics don't help

A diuretic is any drug or substance which makes you urinate more frequently. It will not make you flow more easily, however, and will deplete your body of important vitamins and minerals at a time when you really need them. Coffee is always a irritant, not only because of its caffeine, but because of the many oils and acids it contains. Of course, coffee is also a diuretic. Alcohol is a poison to your body that is all around bad for you, and will make your period worse by increasing water retention.

PMS

For many years premenstrual syndrome, or PMS, was written off as a bunch of psycho-babble on the part of bitchy women who wanted to blame all of their emotional problems on hormonal changes in their bodies.

But tons of medical research later, PMS is widely recognized as a legitimate biological condition with a definite cause associated with the hormonal activities associated with menstruation.

Two hormones come into play to cause PMS. They are estrogen and progesterone. Both of these important body chemicals act up — they increase or dissipate rapidly — and cause irritability and depression, cravings for food, decreased immunity to common illnesses and infections, acne, bloating, weight gain and many other problems.

Some women claim to have PMS for two weeks at a time — the old two weeks on the period and two weeks off. For others it can be just a day or two of upheaval, while still other women have never experienced PMS.

Whatever the cause, there is much you can do, and much you can avoid to lessen your problems with PMS. Let's start with that old nemesis we all love so much, coffee.

Coffee and PMS

According to the American Journal of Public Health, drinking coffee greatly aggravates the symptoms of PMS, including irritability, anxiety, depression, headaches, tender breasts, constipation, acne and cravings for salty and sweet foods.

Drinking coffee just before onset of menstruation is when coffee has its most worst effect, so if you don't want to give up the black stuff altogether, at least stop at the appropriate time of the month.

Alcohol, salt and sugar will also make PMS much worse. Avoid them.

A vegetarian diet may cure you

Never underestimate the power of your diet to affect your mood and the biological balance of your body. High-fat diets with lots of sweets, sugar and alcohol will, without a doubt, make your PMS as bad as it can be. A recent study of vegetarian women showed that women who eat no meat, who have a high-fiber diet, and maintain balanced nutrition, have some 80 percent less PMS than meat-eating women with high fat diets, high sweet diets, and who drink coffee and alcohol.

Don't give in

Perhaps one of the best ways to cope with PMS is to take every symptom it throws at you and turn it into a motivation for positive action. For example, if acne is a symptom, look up some information on healthy skin and see what you can do to treat your skin with tender loving care. Taking positive action of any kind will make you feel better, even if you don't actually conquer the particular symptom. If the symptom is depression, don't try to deny the fact that you are depressed. Acknowledge it, talk it out with someone, or do some tremendous exercising to blast your way through it. When you're depressed, don't get sucked into peripheral thoughts or ideas that contribute to self pity or lead you further into despair. Remember, it may be hormones that make you feel bad, not what your husband or boyfriend is doing. Your hormones are in a constant state of flux. If they made you depressed, they can just as easily bring you back into a light- hearted mood. Always tell yourself: "This, too, shall pass." So whatever the symptom, take direct action. Don't give in. Use the strength of your enemy to defeat it.

The B-6 Cure

Well, perhaps it's not a cure, but all the evidence suggests that if you are deficient in vitamin B-6, you will have a more difficult time with PMS. Here are some high-fiber, vitamin B-6 rich foods that will help you battle PMS:

Kidney beans	sunflower seeds
tuna	white poultry meat
spinach	broccoli
carrots	brussels sprouts
tomatoes	brown rice
peas	potatoes
cauliflower	lima beans
salmon	pearled barley

Finally ...

Be good to yourself during PMS. Get plenty of sleep. Get lots of fresh oxygen through outdoor exercising. Take a lot of hot, quiet baths and try 10 minutes a day of quiet contemplation and meditation. The less stress and the more exercise you have, the lighter your PMS will be.

Multiple Sclerosis

Multiple sclerosis, or MS, is a chronic disease of the nervous system leading to partial paralysis, changes in speech, inability to walk, loss of overall muscle control and more. There is no cure for MS and the disease lasts for many years. Most MS people end up in wheel chairs, although many others retain their ability to walk with ambulatory aides for many years.

Most people with MS require drugs and long-term care from doctors and rehabilitation specialists, such as physical therapists, occupational therapists and others.

While it is difficult to recommend home remedies and things you can do on your own to battle this nightmarish disease, there just may be something you can do for yourself that no doctor or rehab hospital can.

That something is yoga. While yoga is no cure for MS, many people who have MS find that doing yoga not only brings back a tremendous amount of strength and muscle control, but actually holds MS at bay and prevents it from getting worse.

For example, Eric Small is a yoga instructor who has kept his own MS in remission for the past 17 years. Small teaches yoga at the B.K.S. Iyengar Yoga Center in Los Angelas, and he specializes in helping people with MS.

Small starts his students slowly, using props at first to help people support themselves in certain poses, and eventually working up to a point where a prop is no longer needed

The key is to build the muscles slowly, and to keep working the muscles so that they cannot simply give in further to the crippling disease.

In an article in the November/December issue of Yoga Journal, Small said:

"Hatha yoga is effective where physical therapy isn't, in that you become your own teacher. One's breath, mind, and body work together to control physical movement. Using these techniques I have remained symptom free."

If you have MS, don't give in to your disease. A passive attitude toward it will only make your body deteriorate faster. Finding your way into a daily yoga exercise program will be a tremendous boon to you not only physically, but psychologically. As you slowly feel your self growing stronger rather than weaker, you will develop an enormous confidence and sense of hope. Rather than waiting for your body to get worse and worse, you can work toward an ever more livable life despite having a tough disease that most people just give in to. You don't have to.

Muscle Aches and Cramps

If you have achy muscles, and you're just sore all over, it is most likely a minor problem. Some simple common sense things can help you avoid this kind of pain.

For the most part, muscle aches and cramps are the result of poor conditioning, lack of exercise, or exercise that comes only on weekends while the rest of your days are spent sitting at a desk, driving a car or truck, or in front of the television set.

Who is not familiar with the aches and pains after a

weekend of touch football, or tennis, or swimming, or any other exercise that works muscles which haven't been moved in that way in a long time? Well, your body is trying to tell you something. It's telling you that it needs more warning before you put undue stress on it. It means that strenuous exercise only occasionally is not the way to treat yourself. It's telling you that it needs more water and vitamins. Let's look at some specifics:

The warm up

On a zero degree day or colder, you don't get into your car, start it up and take right off — not usually. You let your engine run for a few minutes to warm it up and prevent engine damage. If you're smart enough to give your car a break, you should do the same for your own body. Always do some light exercises and stretching to get your muscles ready for strenuous activity. It will not only prevent muscle aches later, but lessen your chance of injury.

Use ice — it's still good advice

It's as simple as this: wherever your muscles are aching, a cold pack will make it feel a lot better. Ice is a natural anti-inflammatory for overheated muscles. But don't freeze yourself out. If you leave ice on too long, it may interfere with blood flow and result in damage to your muscle tissues. Try a half hour at a time, or for only as long as the pain is troublesome.

Water therapy

Pro athletes all know what makes them feel better after a hard fought game — they sit in a whirlpool bath and let the water work its magic. If you have sore muscles, take to the water yourself. If you don't have a whirlpool or don't have access to one, your bathtub is the next best thing. You can buy devices that cause bath water to circulate if you want to go that route. Taking a warm bath after you have used ice to eliminate swelling and further damage will accelerate the healing process by allowing more blood, oxygen and nutrients into the affected area.

Aspirin and the others

While aspirin is not a good long-term answer to muscle aches, it will certainly help you out when you need it. Aspirin is a natural anti-inflammatory and can reduce swelling and ease pain. The same goes for Tylenol and drugs that contain ibuprofin, such as Nuprin. But don't rely on aspirin and other pills every time you want to do some strenuous activity. It's far better to get in shape with regular exercise so that your body can handle exercise without needing the aid of an artificial anti-inflammatory agent.

The Massage

Few things are better for aching muscles than the application of healing hands to your body, that is, a massage. Muscles respond naturally to the touch of another person, especially when the touch is intended to ease pain and tone the body. You don't have to wait until you need pain relief to get a massage. Make an appointment for a rub down at least once a weak. Your muscles will respond to the stimulus by being more ready and capable to handle bigger jobs, and you'll just feel better in general.

Take your vitamins

Aching muscles may be telling you they are deficient in some important vitamin or mineral. Low amounts of calcium and potassium are well known to cause muscles to cramp up. Especially if you do not eat a well-balanced diet, taking a multi-vitamin supplement may ensure that you have a balance of everything you need. Of course, you're better off improving your diet — making sure you have a lot of fruits and vegetables every day — rather than relying on some "magic pill" to supply your body with everything it needs.

Salute the Sun every morning

Here is a yoga exercise which takes about 5 to 10 minutes, and if you do it every morning, it may provide your body with the total stretch work-out it needs to handle anything for the rest of the day. Most yoga schools call this exercise "Salute the Sun" although it is called other things. Here's how to do it:

(1) Start by just standing up straight with your feet slightly apart with your hands folded together in front of you, as if you were going to pray.

(2) While you inhale, raise your arms over your head and bend slowly backwards from the waist, pushing your pelvis forward/

(3) Now exhale and bend forward and touch the floor with your hands, keeping your knees as straight as you can.

(4) Inhale and bend down on your knees. Still on your knees with your hands on the floor, stretch out your right foot behind you and bend your head back.

(5) Now extend your other foot out so that your hands are on the floor and both your legs are stretched out behind you. At this point, you'll be in a position like you are ready to do some push-ups.

(6) Now, exhaling, lower your body to the floor, knees first, then your forehead and finally your chest.

(7) Now, inhaling, arch your back up, lifting up your head

and letting your pelvis press into the floor.

(8) Exhale as you put your weight on your hands, lift up your butt and raise it high up so that you are making a kind of triangular bridge between your hands and feet.

(9) Now inhale as you bring your right foot forward setting it down between your hands. Keep the left leg extended, raise the head and arch your back.

(10) Exhale now and bring the left leg forward, keep your hand on the floor while you stand back up, so now you are standing and bending over as you were in step three.

(11) Inhale as you stand back up straight raising your arms over your head. Then bend back again as far as you can go.

(12) Exhale as you come back forward lower your arms and relax.

(13) Your can repeat the whole procedure as many times as you want to.

Remember ...

As you know, this is not rocket science. If you stay in shape and follow a regular work-out program, you will have good muscle tone and muscle aches will not be a problem for you. You don't have to have a major exercise or activity, such as a daily basketball game with the boys or a regular aerobics class. Just taking the time to stretch out every day and keeping yourself loose and supple will eliminate muscle pain and cramps. The best way to stay loose and supple is with yogic exercises. The Salute the Sun described above works almost every part of the body. Performing it 10 or 15 times day will be all you need to do to stay in superior shape.

It all goes without saying, although we're going to say it here, that being overweight and having a poor diet will contribute greatly to muscle aches and cramps of all kinds. Stay trim, loose weight and don't put garbage into your body and you won't feel like garbage yourself.

Nausea

If you feel like throwing up, there is probably a good reason for it. But it could be any one of a hundred things. Well, maybe not that many, but think about it. It could be food poisoning, or perhaps just the site of a dead animal on the road. It may be the stomach flu, or simply the violence you are seeing in a creepy movie. A migraine headache can make you vomit, as can an ulcer or an irritable colon. You can get nauseous on a boat, airplane, or even in a car. And as you know, drinking too much beer and having a hangover is probably one of the primary causes of vomiting in America.

Often times, nausea and vomiting is a much needed defense mechanism. If you have swallowed something your body doesn't want, or if you have some virus invading your stomach, the result may be an attempt to throw it out — or in this case — throw it up. So sometimes it's not good to rid yourself of nausea. If your body needs to throw up, let it. It may make you feel better.

But if nausea persists, you should try to determine the cause of the queasiness if you can. If you have the stomach flu, you'll soon realize it because all of the other symptoms of fever, body aches and such will make themselves apparent. In that case, bed rest and limiting your intake of food while the nausea lasts is a good idea. But remember, vomiting leads to dehydration, so as soon as possible, resume intake of liquids.

It would take many pages to cover every single source of nausea and vomiting. So let's look at some general advice to curb nausea, while you keep in mind that the ultimate cause of your nausea needs to be dealt with sooner or later, preferably sooner.

Your mother was probably right

For many years, mothers have been giving their children 7-Up, ginger ale or some other kind of bubbly soda to settle a queasy stomach, and this still may be one of the best remedies. Any sugary or thick syrupy drink can be effective is settling nausea. Also, your mother may have given you toast or crackers. That can be an excellent remedy too.

Check the drug store

You might as well go to the drug store and check out the variety of things they have on their shelves for nausea. Ask your pharmacist for quicker reference. Just remember that Pepto-Bismal will not generally stop your nausea. It and other drugs like it are for stomach problems and diarrhea, and they may not be effective against a queasy stomach.

Maybe it's your ears

Imbalance in the fluid in your ears can cause dizziness and nausea. That's what happens in the case of air sickness or sea sickness. The motion of the vehicle throws off the fluid balance in your ear canals and the result is that sick, queasy feeling. One of the best ways to deal with this problem is to pop a Dramamine, which you can get at any drug store. Don't rely on these as along-term solution, however. If the fluids in your ears are out of balance, and it's not because of motion sickness, then you should see an ear specialist to find out what the problem is.

Gastroenteritis

This is your classic upset stomach and it usually is caused by a virus. Symptoms are nausea, a sore stomach, and vomiting and belching.

Gastro is usually caused by a virus, or it can be something you ate which disagrees with you. Perhaps the best advise for this common condition is to simply wait it out. Gastroenteritis usually resolves itself within 24 hours. Just remember to drink a lot of liquids to counteract dehydration (even if you can't keep it down!) Eventually, you'll settle out and feel better.

Obesity

Weight loss is a major industry in the United States. It is a major obsession for millions of people. There are books upon books upon books on methods to lose weight. There are diets upon diets, pills upon pills, plans upon plans, drinks upon drinks, and exercise programs by the virtual hundreds of thousands — all blaring away at you to lose weight and develop the dream body you have always wanted.

So what can we add to all this that has not already been said somewhere by someone?

It's difficult, it's very difficult.

On the other hand, there are many things we can say for sure:

(1) Losing weight is difficult if you don't get enough exercise.

(2) Counting calories will not do you any good unless you are counting the right kind of calories. When you diet, you should not be eliminating all calories from your food, but only the fat calories. Of all the calories you eat in a given day, less than one-fifth of them should come from fat.

(3) Going on a crash diet is rarely successful and usually ends in failure.

(4) Weight loss programs and drinks almost always end in failure because all the weight lost through these methods is gained back shortly afterwards.

(5) After all the millions of books, program and plans, the common sense approach is still the best!

So now let's put a fresh spin on the common sense of losing weight.

Exercise

Here is why you must exercise to lose weight:

• It burns calories.

• It increases metabolism and muscle. The reason men tend to lose weight faster than women is that men have a higher percentage of muscle than women.

• It promotes fat loss.

• It trims and firms the body.

• It helps control appetite.

• It increases cardiovascular fitness.

• It energizes.

• It takes our minds off food and often improves food choices. After exercising, we're likely to choose low fat foods.

• It makes us feel good and helps our self-esteem.
• It relieves stress and can help you sleep better, especially if the exercise is done outdoors.

When to exercise

The best time to exercise is the time that fits your schedule the most. Some people are morning people and can exercise before going to work. Others feel more energetic at night. It might be easier to exercise before work in the summer when it gets light earlier. Work yourself into what feels good. Some people feel fine with a simple walk. Other don't feel like they have exercised unless they've broken into a sweat.

Okay? So we've established that to lose weight you must exercise, and we've told you why exercise is important and how to get into your own program. Now it's up to you to follow through by choosing your sport — whether it be walking or gymnastics — and sticking to it over the long-term. Now that we've got you moving, lets take a look at eating habits.
Getting rid of excess fat in your diet. Here are 31 ways — one for each day of the month

1. Go ahead, bake a cake and eat it too. But substitute applesauce or low-fat yogurt for butter or oil in your recipe. This works especially well in recipes for darker cakes.

2. Speaking of butter, don't put it on your toast in morning.

Go straight for the preserves. Don't worry, you'll get used to it in just a day or two.

3. A cheese omelet? Are you serious? Go ahead with the omelet but leave out the cheese, and you may also want to use de-cholesteralized eggs or egg whites only. Add onions, garlic and green pepper to your omelet and this will be a breakfast you can live with.

4. When you are eating a piece of fruit while your co-workers are munching on candy and donuts, don't be jealous of them. Don't tell yourself you are being deprived while they enjoy yourselves. Instead remind yourself that you are eating a tasty piece of fruit while they dump fat into their bodies.

5. You wouldn't believe how good chicken pizza with low fat cheese tastes. Avoid greasy pepperoni or, God forbid, sausage. You'd be better of spooning lard into your mouth. Vegetarian pizza is even better than chicken — all the while going extremely easy on the cheese.

6. When you eat salad, you are truly fooling yourself if you put creamy dressings on top, especially blue-cheese. Use just a spot of sesame oil or some extra-virgin olive oil mixed with your favorite spices.

7. Speaking of creaminess, soups such a creamed broccoli or beef soups with little oil spots floating within it are not what you need. Always eat vegetable soups.

8. You wouldn't believe how good a cucumber sandwich is for a brown bag lunch. It's crunchy and tasty and the whole wheat bread will give you a substantial feeling in your stomach.

9. When you eat any kind of sandwich, always avoid buttering the bread and adding mayonnaise. Cranberry

sauce is great on poultry, as is chutney.

10. Use the kind of hot chocolate that mixes with water, not milk.

11. Always eat your popcorn without butter. Salt is no friend to your body either, but only a racoon would eat popcorn without a bit of salt.

12. You can lower your cholesterol level by 100 points in just one month by going completely vegetarian.

13. For cooking or even for drinking, replace regular milk with soymilk. You won't even notice it in your recipes.

14. You will be absolutely amazed at how delicious a sandwich made from a baked red pepper is. Just bake a red pepper in the oven until it's soft. Peal away the skin, cut it into slices and let it cool. Use these thick slices with a bit of onion or garlic and you'll have a zero-fat, excellent sandwich to die... er, to live for.

15. Keep easy-to-eat snacks out of reach. It's so easy to pop 10 or 12 chocolate kisses into your mouth. When you do, you've blown your whole day.

16. When you go to a Chinese restaurant, request that your vegetables be steamed or microwaved, rather than fried in oil in a wok. You'll save untold grams of fat.

17. Eating a lot of beans will curb your craving for fatty meats, and also gives you that comfortable "filled-up" feeling.

18. Here's a much better way to enjoy french fries: cut raw potatoes into french fry sticks, brush them with extra-virgin olive oil and cook them under the broiler for about seven minutes on each side. Eat them with ketchup and

experience what heaven is like. Eat all you want.

19. When you make cookies, use fruit fillings rather than nuts. Nuts are really good for you, but if you really want to eliminate fat from your diet, avoid nuts.

20. You don't have to skip desert, just eat zero-fat deserts. Try a baked apple topped with cinnamon. Have you ever had a baked apple? If you haven't, you haven't lived.

21. Eat all the baked fish you like. The omega-3 oils in it will help you burn fat and cholesterol, even while you're sleeping!

22. Use the water-packed tuna instead of the oil-packed varieties. You'll cut several grams of fat.

23. If you like frozen dinners, read the label and find those that have 10 grams of fat or less. Many of the healthy frozen entrees have as little as 3 grams of fat.

24. Keep the cream and sugar out of your coffee.

25. Did you know that a can of Pepsi has nine teaspoons of dissolved sugar within it? A can of Coke has a mere seven teaspoons of dissolved sugar. You would never sit down and spoon nine teaspoons of sugar into your mouth, would you? So why pour the same down your throat on a 10-minute coffee break?

26. Having fruits and vegetables around is not enough. You should cut them up into chunks, put them on plates and make them easy to grab and ready to eat. Sometimes, the small labor of pealing an orange is enough of a detriment to keep you from eating it. It's so much easier to tear open a candy bar and gobble it down. Ease of access is really the key.

27. What do ground beef, steak, lamb chops, pork chops, chicken, ocean perch, salmon, cheese, whole milk and eggs have in common? They all have zero grams of fiber. Without a lot of fiber, your diet has little chance of succeeding.

28. What do blueberries, brussels sprouts, oat flakes, pumpkins, cooked carrots, brown rice, swiss chard, lettuce, cucumber and applesauce all have in common? They are extremely high fiber foods — all much better sources of fiber than even whole grains. Get as much of these as possible, and your diet will hit the fast track.

29. Instead of scrambled eggs, eat a breakfast of scrambled tofu mixed with chopped onions and sprinkled with pepper and tumeric at least once or twice a week. It will blast many grams of fat away from your diet.

30. Eat small snacks all day rather than three big meals. You'll feel like you're eating more, while actually eating less.

31. Watching television makes you fat in more ways than one. First, sitting there does you little good. Pressing the buttons on the remote burns barely a calorie per hour. But new studies also show that television slows down your body's metabolism. Watching TV puts the body in a hypnotic, deeply relaxed state that slows the body down and makes it less efficient at burning fat. Shut off the TV and go for a walk.

Maintain Common Sense; don't get sucked into easy, expensive diet plans or centers

They say a fool and his money are soon parted. The same could be said of a person who seeks the help of a special diet center, diet pill or diet plan.
Television advertisements hammer away at you all day,

showing you spritely, happy, even downright ecstatic people who used to be fat, but now are thin and beautiful.

We'll put it bluntly: It's all a lie. The hard fact is, all of those people will almost certainly gain their weight back after the commercial has rolled and the cameras and diet center has moved on to the next sucker.

You should just keep telling yourself every day: "The only true way to lose weight is to exercise more, and eat less fat, and to do so continuously for the rest of my life."

Other sources of obesity

It should be mentioned that some people gain weight not because of poor eating habits or lack of exercise. Some obesity is caused by biochemical imbalances in the body or some other disease.

Some of those conditions include diseases of the endocrine glands, such as thyroid disorders or diabetes. Disorders that affect the area of the brain that controls your desire to eat can also be at the root of the problem. If you think one of these condition may be the source of your weight problem, see a doctor for an evaluation.

Also, many medications can lead to obesity. If you are taking any kind of prescription drug, ask your doctor about potential side effects as far as weight loss is concerned. Birth control pills and cortisone tablets are likely suspects in unexplained weight gain.

One other thing: There's a definite link between depression and weight gain. It may be more than just feeling too depressed to get up an do something about the condition of your body. If you have Seasonal Affective Disorder (SAD) your regular winter weight gain may be due to the fact that you are not getting enough sunshine. Not having enough sun may trigger a sort of "hibernation" state in your body, making you sluggish, more hungry for fat and sweets or other filling foods that might make you feel warmer in the cold weather. If it is winter time and you are feeling inexplicably depressed and putting on the pounds, turn to the "Depression" section in this book and see the heading under SAD for information on how to defeat this problem.

Osteoporosis

Osteoporosis, or thinning of the bones, affects about 24 million Americans, most of them women. About 40 percent of all American women are expected to develop some form of osteoporosis in their lifetimes. Some 1.3 million women a year suffer fractures because of osteoporosis. About $10 billion per year in medical costs is accounted for by this disease.

Even so, it is clear that every single person in danger of developing osteoporosis can prevent it from happening by making changes in their diet, and by avoiding harmful substances which contribute to the disease.

As you probably know, osteoporosis results primarily from calcium deficiency. Women who do not get enough calcium from an early age have a tremendously bigger chance of bone thinning later in life.

Most people reach maximum bone mass in their bodies between the ages of 35 and 45. After that it's all down hill. Bones began to get thinner, and those bones that have not had adequate calcium to bulk them up early on will thin much faster, leading to all the painful symptoms of osteoporosis, which include bone fractures, broken hips, bent posture, inability to walk and other problems. People with osteoporosis also have more infections and embolisms, which are an obstruction of an artery caused by blockages in the bones. Sometimes even a sudden movement or a heavy sneeze can result in a cracked rib or broken bone.

Here are the people that are most at risk for developing osteoporosis:

- Small people with petite frames
- White, light and fair-haired people with ancestry from Europe or the far east.
- People who do little or no exercise
- Women who have never given birth
- People who are lactose intolerant
- People with low body fat
- All women over 40
- Women who have had their ovaries removed
- Women who have had an early menopause

Let's look at some things you can do to prevent osteoporosis from happening to you

Exercise

You already know that regular exercise makes your muscles bigger, tougher and stronger. The same is true of your bones. Exercising also makes your bones thicker and more healthy. Not exercising at all means your bones will stay thin or gradually deplete themselves. If you have a sedentary lifestyle and you just don't like to move around, you are putting yourself at great risk later in life, not only for osteoporosis, but for other diseases as well, such as heart disease, hypertension and others. The sooner you start an exercise regime the better. Remember that osteoporosis takes many years to develop and every year you add to your exercise program helps a lot.

Getting the calcium you need

Of course, the best source of calcium in is in dairy products, especially milk. But drink skim milk to avoid the harmful by-products of milk, such as cholesterol and sodium. Milk is not the only source of calcium, however. Here are some other foods that contain large amount of the stuff:

baked beans	sardines with bones
low-fat yogurt	beet greens
broccoli	collard greens
mackerel	salmon with bones
mustard greens	cottage cheese
oysters	okra
scallops	tofu
turnip greens	ice milk

Many breakfast cereals now fortify their products with calcium. These are an excellent source, especially if you eat your cereal with a glass of skim milk.

Take a calcium supplement

With all the clamor about osteoporosis in the media of late, calcium supplements have sprouted up on the market faster than weeds in a wet ditch. Taking calcium supplements on a regular basis will help maintain your calcium levels, especially if you are allergic to milk and other dairy products. Be aware, though, that studies show that absorption of calcium from supplements is inferior to that from natural sources in your food. Don't rely on them completely. If you are allergic to dairy products, some of the other foods listed above will provide you the calcium you need.

More vitamin D, too

Vitamin D helps your body absorb calcium. You could be getting all the calcium you need, but without the ability of your body to take it in, it won't do you much good. One of the easiest way to get vitamin D is to go outside and get a little sunshine. The sun striking your skin sets up a chemical reaction in your body that stimulates the production of vitamin D. Too much sun, however, is harmful, so getting your D this way is not a complete answer. Fish is a good source of vitamin D, especially tuna, mackerel, sardines and salmon. Many dry cereals and milk also contain vitamin D.

Smoking, alcohol and caffeine

Yes, here they are again. These three evil products are behind so many diseases in the human body, it shouldn't surprise you to hear that they also contribute to bone thinning. The more of them that you avoid, and the longer you avoid them, the better off you'll be.

Remember...

Osteoporosis is one of those diseases that which, once you reach the point of no return, there is very little medical science can do for you. One of four women who suffer a major fracture due to osteoporosis never leave the hospital or nursing home again. Take care of yourself now, long before you ever get to that position.

Pneumonia

Pneumonia is basically inflammation of the lungs. Most likely the cause of pneumonia is not a single thing, but many. There are specific pneumonia germs, but this disease can also result from influenza, staph or strep infections, some kind of virus or even parasites, chemical agents and allergies.

People with pneumonia have a very bad cough and will often cough up blood or other sputum that can be green, yellow or rust colored. Fever always accompanies the onset of pneumonia and you may also have shaking and chills. In the early stages, you will experience a sharp pain in the chest when you take a deep breath.

It is important to note that pneumonia can be mistaken for a bad cold that "doesn't want to go away." People sometimes call this "walking pneumonia."

If you have pneumonia, it will likely kill you unless you get treatment, and that means powerful antibiotics from a doctor.

A vaccine is available for certain kinds of pneumonia, and if you are at a high risk for developing the disease, the vaccine may be for you, although it may not provide you with "immunity" to pneumonia.

If you have had a cold or flu that seems to have hung around forever, if you have a cough that's getting worse and worse and you're starting to cough up blood or mucus, if you are feeling extremely "sick all over" and you have a fever, don't fool around. Get yourself to a doctor before you suffer permanent lung damage or die.

Remember, pneumonia can infect those around you, so taking action as quickly as possible will not only help yourself, but prevent dangers to others.

Poisoning

Most people who are poisoned are children. That's because they are curious and tend to put things in their mouths, especially things that look good to them, such as a bottle of shiny pink pills that might look like candy. In fact, the most common kind of poisoning in the U.S. is too many aspirins taken by children. The obvious solution is to inspect your home now to make sure your children do not have access to where the aspirins or other hazardous stuff is stored.

Lot's of people — children and adults — are poisoned every year by a variety of substances, including solids, liquids and gases. You can also be poisoned by food which has gone bad, even if it tastes okay. Botulism is a particularly fatal form of poisoning, caused by the germ clostridium botulinum, and it is most often found in canned food and spoiled meat. If a person has ingested the butulism germ, you must get the victim to the hospital as soon as possible because this poisoning can kill within minutes. Avoid eating foods from cans that have been dented or damaged. Even a microscopic break in the can's integrity can let it harmful bacteria.

No matter what the poison, here is a procedure to follow in the event it happens to you or someone near you:

(1) The most common poisoning is something that someone has swallowed. The best bet it to dilute the poison with a large intake of water or milk. This will reduce the potency of whatever has been swallowed by thinning it out. Also, many common poisons substances have instructions on the label about which antidote will be most effective if the substance has been accidentally swallowed.

(2) Induce vomiting, except when what has been swallowed is some kind of acid or tissue-burning substance, like drain cleaner or gasoline. Vomiting can be triggered with a finger down the throat, or with syrup of ipecac, which you can buy at a drug store.

Other times when inducing vomiting is not recommended:

• When a person is convulsing.

• In an infant under six months age.

• In a child who has swallowed a hard material object.

• When a large dose of sleeping pills has already made a person drowsy.

(3) Mustard mixed with water is called a "universal antidote." Have the victim swallow as much of this and more water as possible.

(4) Make sure the patient keeps breathing or supply emergency breathing and CPR if necessary.

(5) Call the nearest poison control center. Look up the number on the emergency page of your local directory or call 911. You should have the number of the poison control center posted near the telephone along with other emergency numbers.

Power Line Alert!

(Is your electric blanket making you sick?)

If you and your whole family — even your nearby neighbors — find yourself constantly involved with a lot of health problems, your bodies may be reacting to harmful electromagnetic currents radiating from nearby power lines.

The dangers from power line, radar and visual display terminals are more and more being looked at by scientists for their adverse effect on health.

Scientists now believe that electromagentic radiation, or EM, in the environment interacts dangerously with the body's own electrical currents, disturbing brain chemistry, biological clocks and the immune system. The result can be numerous and persistent illness of all kinds. including deadly cancer or a general state of ill health or symptoms of Alzheimer's Disease and dementia.

Some of the EM sources can also come from sources right inside your home. Your warm and comfortable electric blanket, for example, may be reaking havoc on the natural flow of your body currents by bathing you in a blanket of harmful EM. Many new studies have found increased levels of cancer in people living near high-voltage power lines; telephone lineworkers, subway drivers and electricians.

Radar has also been linked to cancer because it increases the activity of an enzyme called ornithine decarboxylase. People residing near Air Force early-warning radar systems have shown dramatically increased levels of cancer.

Computer screens have been linked to birth defects among

women who work with compuetrs all day in offices.

The solution is to simply take yourself out of harms way. If your house or apartment is in close proximity to large powerlines or other powerful electrical structures, you should consider moving. Try giving up your electric blanket, or any other stong source of EM radiation in your home. Those who work all day on computers can buy devices that sit next to your machine and thwart EM radiation before it gets to your body. Ask your computer dealer about where to buy such a device.

Ridding your environement of EM radiation may be the very key you have been looking for in your life. It may be the single thing that is standing in the way of a pain-free life of vibrant health and mental alertness. Check it out!

Prostate Problems

One of the most common forms of cancer in older men is prostate cancer. But another common prostate problem is known as benign prostatic hyperplasia (BPH). It attacks about half of all men older than age 55, and is basically the enlargement of the prostate gland.

The prostate gland is located just below the bladder, and it surrounds part of the urethra, the tube through which urine flows.

Men who have BPH experience problems urinating. They may have trouble starting, stopping or may often feel like they have to go when they don't. BPH is not life threatening like prostate cancer, but it can lead to many other problems, such as bladder infection, kidney problems and sexual disfunction.

One of the biggest contributors to BPH is probably a high fat diet. Men with BPH measure cholesterol levels and average of 80 percent higher than men without the disease. Alcohol and stress also may contribute to the development of BPH.

About 300,000 men per year have surgery to correct enlarged prostates, but many of those surgeries may be unnecessary. There are many natural remedies that you can find in health food stores that will shrink your prostate, if BPH is the cause. (Note: Only a doctor can tell the difference between BPH and prostate cancer, so get a firm diagnosis before you go ahead with natural remedies).

Here are some natural herbs and vitamins that have been shown to shrink the prostates of men with BPH, according to David Steinman, author of Diet for a Poisoned Planet.

Saw Palmetto — This decreases the frequency of urination and eases inflammation of BPH. Should be taken twice daily.

Zinc — Studies show it reduces the symptoms of BPH. One supplement a day to treat BPH.

Amino Acids — This combination of amino acids relieves BPH: glycine, l-lalanine and l-glutamic acid. Ask your health food vender for advice about dosage.

Ginseng — This common diet supplement, which many people use to enhance sexual desire and performance, can decrease the size of the prostate. Ginseng increases the level of the male hormone, testosterone, in the body, which improves zinc absorption.

Horsetail — Reduces inflammation due to BPH. Ask your health food dealer or herbologist about dosage.

Bee Pollen — This has been used to treat BPH in Europe for more than 30 years .Two teaspoons should be taken daily.

Many men have used the above, both individually or in combination, to successfully treat BPH. The advantage of using these natural remedies is avoiding the side effects of prescription drugs for BPH.   One common BPH drug, Proscar, for example, has been known to cause impotence in a small percentage of men as well as decreases in sexual drive.

All of the above natural remedies are available in any health food store, and some stores will carry pre-mixed version of the above in one, easy-to-eat supplement capsule. These supplements cost about half as much as prescriptions from your doctor for prostate swelling.

Remember, see your doctor for a proper diagnosis. Make sure you do not have prostate cancer, rather than BPH.

Special Report:
How to talk to your doctor

If you had a migrain headache, why would you seek out a gastroenterologist, a doctor who specializes in stomach disorders?

Hundreds of people do! Why? Because some headaches are severe enough to cause vomiting and abdomincal aches, and many people assume that their stomach is the problem and not their head!

You can't always assume a doctor is going to tell you different. If you go to a doctor and complain of vomiting and stomach cramps, he/she may treat you for that when, in reality, you need something for a headache!

The above is just one example of how obvious medical problems can be misinterpreted.
The fact is, one of the most difficult things for any doctor to do is to find what's wrong with you. Diagnostics, as it is called, is a science in itself, and many books have been written on that subject alone.

In order for a doctor to provide you with the correct treatment or to prescribe the right drug, he or she has to have some way of communicating with you in a way that is clear, meaningful, and which leaves little room for misunderstanding. It's just common sense — if you don't give accurate information to your doctor, how can he prescribe the proper treatment? Let's take a closer look at this important subject.

Ten Tips on how to talk to your doctor

Tip One: Nothing is too personal!

Sometimes, being totally open and honest, even when your life depends on it, can be an incredibly difficult thing to do. Many people, for example, will be hesitant to confide to their doctor that they may have a sexually transmitted disease, or that a member of their family is having problems with delusions or insanity.

Remember that a doctor "sees it all" almost everyday. If you tell your doctor you think you might have syphyliss or herpes, he or she won't bat an eye. It is not their job to judge you! It's their job to heal you. In order to do that, they need the truth from you.

Tip Two: Don't try to diagnose yourself

Many people go to a doctor after having given a lot of thought to what they think is wrong with them. Many have even reached a conclusion in their minds about what's wrong with them. But you should let the doctor make his own decision. He or she does it every day for a living, has spent 10 years in school learning how to do it and has a lot of experience with discovering medical problems. (Note: don't take this too far, however. Always reserve your right to question your doctor, even doubt him/her. Sometimes being too passive in a doctor-patient relationship is one of the worst ways to get to the bottom of your medical probelm.)

Tip Three: Be prepared with a complete, accurate family history

Sometimes a doctor's examination, blood tests, X-rays and other diagnostic devices aren't enough to provide a complete picture of what might be wrong with you. Telling your doctor about your family history may be the best source, and provide the key to a proper diagnosis, especially if there is a condition in your family that is genetically generated and has a high probablity of being repeated.

Tip Four: Don't use medical terminology with your doctor

A frequent source of improper diagnosis happens when a patient uses medical terms in the wrong sense. Talk to your doctor in simple everyday terms. These days we are all inundated with medical information from the media — books, magazines, newspapers, radio, television — and much of the time this can be a great source of misuderstanding of medical terms on behalf of the public. Remember, many medical programs are primarily venues of entertainment, not serious medical care.

Tip Five: A simple idea: Point to where it hurts!

A person complaining of a pain in the chest or stomach may be suffering from any number of ailments. The chest or the stomach are not particularly large surface areas, there are literally an infinite number of spots on any human body where a medical problem can be pinpointed. As we saw in Rule One above, a stomach ache can be the result of a pain in the head. A pain in the chest may be on the right side just below the shoulder blade, or on the left side just below the rib cage — but your doctor won't know until you actually point to just the right spot!

Tip Six: Keep in mind unusual activities or circumstances

Have you been recently engaged in some activity or been somewhere you don't normally go? Have you eaten a new kind of food, or tasted something you've never tried before. This may be the key to a sudden, mysterious change in your health. Think hard. Where have you been or what have you done differently recently that may have made you ill.   If you can think of something, even if it seems irrelevant, tell your doctor about it. This may provide the very clue that is needed to solve the puzzle of what's wrong with you.

Tip Seven: Don't let your child describe his/her own symptoms

For obvious reasons, a child may have many reasons to mislead a docotor. Children are easily frightended and confused by medical people and environments, and they may say anything a parent or doctor wants them to say. Even more than adults, children may use terms they don't understand, which can add to the confusion.

Tip Eight: Let your doctor talk to your spouse

The one person most people will share their most private and personal feelings with is their spouse. Often times a husband or wife can be more objective about you than you can be about yourself. If you are facing a daunting medical problem and have had little success after talking to many doctors, have your spouse talk to a doctor in private. It's amazing how often this can lead to a more honest and accurate assessment of what is going on with a person's health.

Tip Nine: Don't be a doctor doormat!

Traditionally the doctor-patient relationship has been one of "master and slave." It shouldn't be that way. A doctor is not an omnipotent God that knows all. In the not-so-recent past, doctors were never questioned or second-guessed by anyone, including nurses, technicians, and least of all, the patient. This approach can be counterproductive for both you and the doctor. Respect a doctor for what they are and what they know, but don't be totally passive to their every statement or suggestion. Take an active part in your own diagnosis and decisions about your treatment. If your doctor doesn't care for your input — fire him! After all it's your body and your life. Ultimately, you are the one who is in control, and you bear the responsibility for your health.

Tip Ten: If your doctor recommends surgery ALWAYS get a second opinion!

At times the number of unnecessary surgeries done in this country reached epidemic proportions.   The economic incentive for a physician to operate on you is great. Surgeries make doctors a lot of money.   Doctors are human beings and they are not immune to the lure of bigger profits. Whenever a doctor recommends surgery, you should take the time and trouble to go to   another doctor for a fresh perspective. Avoiding an unnecessary surgery could save your life and save you thousands of dollars! It's worth the time to get a second opinion.

Ringing in the ears (tinnitus)

Ringing in the ears is also known as tinnitus. It most often effects older people. Ringing is not the only kind of noise people hear with this condition. Buzzing, hissing, roaring or clicking noises are also common.

The two most common cause of tinnitus are wax in the ear canal, or exposure to a loud noise.

If you're lucky, a good cleaning of the ears will rid you of the problem. This does not mean swabbing yourself with a Q-Tip — in fact, that's about the worst thing you can do. It's actually Q-Tips that probably caused the problem in the first place, that is, it's how you use a Q-Tip that causes the problem.

Many people attempt to clean their ears by moving a cotton swab around and around in their ear.   The result is that some wax is pushed further back into the ear where it builds up and hardens. That's how problems develop. It's better to clean your ear without use of a swab. Go to your drug store and by some ear cleaning solution. Read the instructions and place the solution in your ear. Lay down on the opposite ear for 10-15 minutes to let it dissolve the wax in your ear. Then turn over and drain your ear on a cloth or paper towel. Do the same for the other ear. You may have to do this several times to get the ear completely clean.

Having clean ears may rid you of tinnitus.

If it doesn't, you may have a problem that was generated by a sudden loud noise, or frequent exposure to high levels of sound. If that's the case, the sound will eventually go away on its own accord, or you will need surgery to correct the problem. Be warned, however, that there really is no sure-fire cure for tinnitus. If you have done everything you can to relieve the noise in your ears to no avail, then your only alternative may be to buy a device that masks the sound. Such devices can be purchased in a drug store or health care supply store. They are called tinnitus maskers and fit inside your ear much like a hearing aid. They generate a pleasant sound which drowns out the noise of your tinnitus. It's probably not the total silence you wish for, but it will be better than the noise of tinnitus.

Seizures

The good news about seizures is that 90 percent of them can be prevented from ever happening.

But when they do happen, especially major seizures, they can be incredibly frightening. People can suddenly start to shake, flail around, foam at the mouth, jerk around and go unconscious. Many people also hurt themselves in the process of a seizure. A head injury is common during a seizure as a result from falling down or banging against some object.

Seizures are usually caused by some problem in the brain. That can be scars on the brain produced by a past injury, abnormal electrical activity in the brain, or from other factors which may effect brain functioning. Some of those are strokes, heart disease, kidney trouble, sinus infection, ear problems, high fever, or poisoning from too much alcohol, caffeine or drugs.

Sometimes a seizure can be brought on by a night of hard drinking, very little sleep and then a load of coffee or "pep pills," such as NoDoz or Vivarin the next morning. If you abuse your body that way, it's bound to react by trying to shake you up a bit — or a lot.

Despite the possibility of injury during the actual event, seizures usually leave the victim unharmed, and perhaps just tired and dazed. Of course, suffering a seizure while driving a car or operating some other heavy machinery is a sure formula for disaster.

If you have had a seizure, you should always assume that you could have another one some day, even though that may never happen. People who have had seizures should always make sure they get enough sleep every night, and should take strenuous steps to avoid mood altering chemicals, such as alcohol and caffeine.

Sometimes high stress combined with lots of coffee and a poor diet can set the stage for a seizure, so it's important for seizure prone people to take it easy, keep the stress off their jobs or lives at a minimum and to eat good food and get adequate rest.

Of course, if you have some other condition, such as

diabetes, then you should be taking all of the precautions that go along with treating that illness. Otherwise, you are asking for trouble.

The only other alternative are drugs prescribed by a doctor, but many of these have unpleasant side effects. Those side-effects may be worth it, however, if you have a problem with major seizures that occur frequently.

Here's what to do when someone has a seizure

(1) Make sure the victim has an open airway. This can most often be accomplished by rolling the person on his or her side. If their is vomit in the mouth, clear it out with your finger.

(2) If cuts or broken bones result, bind them up or splint them as best you can with your available resources.

(3) Make the victim as comfortable as possible.

(4) Once the seizure has ended, take the person to the hospital, preferably by ambulance as soon as possible.

Sexuality

A lot of people will tell you that there are no such things as real aphrodisiacs — foods, drugs, herbs or special preparations that will stimulate sexual desire or improve sexual performance.

But many people believe that certain substances are aphrodisiacs. Perhaps the most common is ginseng, which is especially popular in Oriental countries and cultures. And there may be something to, especially for females. A daily dose of ginseng extract, or ginseng tea is known to increase the level of testosterone in males. Testosterone of course is the "male hormone" and having a higher level of it may increase a man's libido and stamina in sexual activity.

Other more exotic substances are frequently sought for their purported aphrodisiacal properties, notable, powdered rhinoceros horns. In fact, the rhinoceros is being hunted to extinction because the demand for their horns is so high in China that many people are willing to take the great risk or poaching rhinos.

Like ginseng, however, powdered rhino horn is probably not an aphrodisiac.

But to say there are no aphrodisiac is not entirely true either. Several drugs, for example, clearly work with the human body chemistry to stimulate sexual function. The prescription drug bromocriptine (brand name is Parlodel) is very effective in reversing male impotency, and has been shown to increase libido by 80 percent in both males and females. Bromocriptine has also been know to return post-menopausal women to regular mentrual cycles, even women in their 60s and 70s!

Another prescription drug that increases sexual function is called Diapid, which is a synthetic version of the hormone vasopressin — a natural human hormone. Diapid prolongs and intesnifies orgasms.

Of course, to obtain these drugs you must get a prescription from a doctor, and they are also probably not long-term solutions to sexual problems, nor will they likely contribute to a healthy sex life in the long run.

What you can do to improve your sex life

But there is good news. Research has clearly shown that

certain vitamins play an important role in increasing and enhancing sexuality. These foods may not be "love potions" or aphrodisiacs per say, but they do help along the chemicals in your brain — called neurotransmitters — which are needed for healthy sexual functioning.

Vitamin B-5 (also known as calcium pantothenate) may be able to inrease your sexual stamina, if you take it with lecithin and choline, both common items you can purchase in health food stores.

Another B vitamin, Niacin, or Vitamin B-6 plays an extrememly important role in attaining orgasm. A chemical in your body called histamine, which has many functions, is closely associated with orgasm release. An amino acid called histidine in your body is converted into histamine by niacin. Niancin causes the release of histimine — which produces the flushed itching feeling often associated with orgasm.

Taking niacin supplements about a half hour or so before having sex may assist in your ability to have an orgasm. Also, making sure you are getting enough niacin in your diet may help insure you have the ability to have an orgasm whenver you want to. These foods are high in niancin, and therefore, may help sexual function:

Tuna (water packed)	mackeral
chicken breast	pink salmon
veal rump roast	Kaboom (cereal)
turkey breast	Product 19 (cereal)
cod	crabmeat
lamb	Quaker Instant Oatmeal

Sinusitis

Sinusitis is an infection of the sinus cavities around your eyes and nose. There are eight sinus cavities in all. The ones most prone to infection are the two frontal sinus cavities in the forehead and the two in the cheekbones.

Infection in these or other sinus cavities can result in yellow or green discharge from the nose, swelling around one or both of the eyes, a pounding headache, pain when you press on the side of your nose, possible pain in the teeth, a low-grade fever, a feeling of pressure in your head when you bend over, and a constant dripping in the back or your throat that makes you cough.

Children don't often suffer from sinusitis because their sinus cavities are not very well developed.

For those adults who suffer from this painful and irritating disease, a night of trying to sleep can end up being like the Chinese water torture — a constant drip, drip, drip of nasal fluid down your throat.

Sinusitis effects about 50 million people per year. It's caused by allergies or other sources of swelling which lead to the eventual trapping of bacteria, which grow and multiply in your nose. Because sinusitis is primarily a bacterial infection, the best way to treat it is with anti-biotics.

But you can prevent yourself from ever getting to the point where you need a doctor to prescribe medicine for you. The best way to battle sinus infection is to eliminate the conditions that make bacterial growth possible.

Reduce swelling with hot and cold

Swelling is what creates closed, moist pockets which are breeding grounds for bacteria. Steamy vapors are excellent for opening up blocked sinuses, and allowing them to drain. Get yourself to a vaporizer several times a day to keep things flowing. Also, you may try alternating hot and cold compresses to stimulate the flow of mucus.

Salt water and baking soda

At first you may not like the idea of sticking salt water up your nose, but a mixture of salt water and baking soda is an excellent remedy for flushing out infected nasal passages. Mix one teaspoon of table salt with two cups of warm water and just a pinch of baking soda. Sniff the mixture into your nose one nostril at a time and then gently let it back out.

Also, gargling with a warmer version of the same mixture every three hours will have a beneficial effect.

A jolt of Java

Steamy hot coffee will help dilate your nostrils an the caffeine may help constrict the blood vessels in your nose. Obviously you shouldn't drink coffee all day, but when you need some quick relief, a nice mug of hot Java can feel pretty darned good.

Popping the pills

Take an over-the-counter nasal decongestant pill to help shrink swollen membranes, and you can also take an aspirin or two to relieve pain.

More fluids

Just as fluids help with the cold and flu, drinking lots of liquids will increase the flow of your sinuses.

Your key to quitting?

There are few things which aggravate the sinus cavities more than the filmy wisps of the demon weed going up your nose and into your throat. Smoking will make sinus infections worse, perhaps even dangerously so. Quit smoking when you have a sinus infection and then don't start up again.

Finally, spice up your life

You know that feeling you get when you eat a super-hot burrito or a bowl of 15-alarm chili? It sort of blows your windpipes out and sends a rush through your nose. Well, the same affect may be helpful in dilating your sinuses. Hot spices, garlic and raw onions can really get your mucous membranes going. Garlic is even a natural, mild antibiotic, so taking some of this pungent stuff can put your healing on the fast-track.

Sleeping

It's not necessarily how much or how little sleep you get — it's getting the amount of sleep you need to help you function properly ...and that may be more or less than others. Generally, a person has insomnia if his or her ability to sleep interferes chronically with daytime functioning. Some people get by fine with four hours of shut-eye, while others need a solid 10 hours to function normally. If you don't get the amount you need, then you have insomnia

The causes of insomnia can be many and difficult to pinpoint. Too much anxiety, depression, too much coffee, too little to eat, over eating to name just a few.

Whatever the cause, the following 10-point sleep program will help you get the proper amount of rest that's right for you.

A 10-point Program for Better Sleep

(1) Sleep as much as you need to feel refreshed and healthy during the following day, but no more or no less. Cutting down sleep time slightly can lead to better, deeper sleep. Trying to sleep too long, on the other hand, may result in fragmented or shallow sleep.

(2) A regular arousal time in the morning seems to strengthen cicadian cycling and to finally lead to regular times of sleep onset.

(3) A steady, daily amount of exercise probably deepens sleep in the long run, but sometimes one-shot exercise does not directly influence sleep during the following night.

(4) Occasional loud noices, such as aircraft or loud trucks, disturb even sleepers who do not awaken and cannot remember them in the morning. So if you sleep next to excessive noise, do something to soundproof your room, or find a room that's more quiet.

(5) Although and excessively warm room disturbs sleep, there is no evidence that a cold room helps sleep, as many people believe. Just don't have it too hot in the room.

(6) Hunger may disturb sleep. A light bedtime snack, especially warm milk (which truly is a mild sedative) can

help you get to sleep.

(7) Avoid sleeping pills. You'll soon become addicted to them. Also, the drugs in sleeping pills may interfere with dreaming and other normal sleep activities, which can leave you just as tired after you wake up.

(8) Avoid caffeine, especially after 5 p.m. Even people who do not feel the effects of caffeine can have their sleep disturbed by this jitter-bug drug.

(9) Alcohol may help you fall asleep faster, but it will almost certainly wake you up a short while later and make you feel jittery. Alcohol will ruin your sleep, not help it.

(10) Rather than trying very hard to sleep on a night when you can't, you might be better off turning on a light and doing something else for a half hour or so. Trying to sleep when you can't can be very frustrating and stressful. The result is even more sleep disturbance. Turning on the TV is probably not a good idea. You may fall asleep in front of it, but sleeping in front of a television is not a quality way to sleep.

Don't worry

If you can't fall asleep as you lie in bed, don't worry about it. Just being in bed is a form of rest, and you may be getting more sleep than you realize. Often times, we drop off and wake up again without knowing it, and the result may be more sleep than you think you are getting.

Don't count sheep, count your breaths

One of the most common causes of insomnia is a mind that races and refuses to shut up when it's time for bed. You know the feeling.

But you can get control of your mind by giving yourself this task: Tell yourself that you will think of nothing else but the motion of your breathing. Also, you will count your breaths up to four times, and then begin again.
In other words, count one inhale and one exhale as "one" — the next inhale and exhale as "two" — and so on, up to four inhales and exhales until you get to four. When you get to four, start over again at one.

Make a game of it. See how well you can think of nothing — absolutely nothing — except the number of your breaths.
It's as simple as that. Counting your breaths is an incredibly effective method of clearing your mind and falling asleep. It's not likely you'll get through more than two or three cycles of four before you're fast asleep.

Take your vitamins

Some sleep disorders are associated with a lack of certain vitamins and minerals in your diet. Taking a daily multi-vitamin may be all you need to make sure you get all the nutrients you need to get to sleep. Also, look into copper and iron deficiencies. Not having enough of these two minerals can make you lose sleep.

Iron

A good source of iron — almonds and raisins. Munch on almonds before bedtime with glass of warm milk and you may fall asleep where you sit.

Copper

A good source of copper — clams. Yes, clams. But swallowing a few slimy clams may not be your idea of an excellent nighttime snack (or anytime snack). Apricots are a moderately good source of copper, as is whole wheat pasta and Grape Nuts cereal. In fact, a bowl of Grape Nuts with warm milk and some raisins would be a superb sleep aid!

Skin Rashes & Diseases

A rash is a general term that could be used to describe everything from hives to poison ivy, or even measles.

Anything that makes you itch, break out, burn, or chaff is something affecting your skin from an internal or external source. Most skin conditions are transitory, lasting only minutes before they clear up on their own accord. Other are persistent, and some can point to a more serious disease within your system

Let's look at some common skin condition one at a time and see what we can do about them.

Dermatitis and Eczema

These two terms are sometimes used interchangably. In fact, there are many different kinds of each, if you really want to get technical about it. But in general, you would be safe to say that dermatitis and eczema are inflammations of the skin, characterized by excessive dryness, cracks, blisters, crusty and sometimes oozing.

The causes can be as simple as washing too many dishes or dry winter weather, or as complex as a systemic problem with your body chemistry.

The good news about dermatitis and eczema? It's not contagious. Often times this condition is the result of something you come into contact with, such as burning weed, ragweed, poison ivy — or just about anything you are sensitive or allergic to.

Best Advice?

Be very cognizant about maintaining the moisture in your skin, and avoiding those things which dry out your skin. If you wash too many dishes, keep the water away from your hands with rubber gloves. If you live in a high, cold, dry wintry climate, frequent use of skin moisturizer will help you out. Obviously, cold, hard winds can be murder on your skin, so wrap up and protect exposed areas.

If you have some sort of contact dermatitis, such as a reaction to a plant or substance, get a good hydrocortisone cream from the drugstore — they're very effective. Also, taking an oral antihistamine will fight off the reaction. Needless to say, if you have a known allergy, avoid whatever it is that trips your trigger.

Baking Soda Bath ... then hit the Aloe Vera

A good 15- to 20-minute soaking in a bath with a half-cup of baking soda in it will do wonders for your skin. First of all, soaking for more than 10 minutes allows a deeper layer of your skin to be penetrated by moisture, which will help soften it up in general. The baking soda adds a mild medicinal effect. Baking soda can be far more refreshing and less messy than application of creams and tar solutions.

When you get out of the tub, use a skin cream with aloe vera as a primary ingredient. Recent studies show that aloe vera contains many naturally occuring anti-inflammatory agents. Dry your skin comepletely before applying an aloe vera cream. You can also get your aloe directly from an aloe plant, although to get the amounts you need, an off-the-shelf product is no doubt more useful.

Keep up with it

Don't give your skin a chance to get worse and worse. While your areas of infection are still localized, attack them with cortisone and moisturizing creams before collateral damage of the skin occurs. Don't forget to apply creams and moisutizers before you go to bed. This can be messy, but it may help you stay ahead of the problem and clear it up faster.

Dermatitis and eczema can be more of minor pain and irritant than anything, but treating yourself will ensure that something worse doesn't develop, such as skin infection.

Hives

Just what are hives? They are an allergic condition of the skin characterized by the formation of large blotches or welts which itch intensely. Hives arise on your skin when you eat something you are allergic to, when you come into contact with a skin-sensitive substance, or can even be produced by the overheating of your body.

The best way to get rid of them is to avoid or remove that substance which caused them. If you don't know what caused your hives, you may have an allergy you still don't know about. See the section under "Allergy" to find out more about discovering your possible aversions.

Hives usually go away of their own accord, so just wait them out. Creams and cortisone treatments will definitely help, but are probably not necessary. Even an aspirin might help because it is an anti-inflammatory drug.

Psoriasis

This disease is a gigantic nightmare for millions of people. Psoriasis is a baffling skin disease with no known cause and no known cure. Psoriasis is the result of skin cells reproducing so rapidly that they cannot be cast off fast enough from the surface of your skin. The result is a crusty buildup of silvery-white patches of skin that are very resistent to most remedies.

The good news is that psoriasis is not contagious. Also, those who have it may be nearly immune to skin cancer. Recent studies of skin cancer victims showed that people with proriasis have a nearly 100 percent less chance of contracting skin cancer than non-psoriasis sufferers who have spent an equal amount of time working out in direct sunlight.

While psoriasis is tough to deal with, not dealing with it at all can be the worst thing you can do. Psoriasis almost always gets worse and worse, and can spread from the place where it starts. Often times, the key is to attack psoriasis while it effects only a small patch of skin.

Over the counter products

Most over-the-counter products rely on coal-tar solutions in varying percentages to fight psoriasis. The stronger the percentage of coal-tar in the cream or shampoo, the better, although you may not need the strongest from the beginning. Another common psoriasis medication is salycilic acid, which can be found in a number of products.

But you'll have to experiment on your own. What works for one prosiasis sufferer, is not at all effective for another. Also, one of the most baffling things about psoriasis is that a medication that works one day may stop working the next. The disease seems able to adjust to agents which tend to counteract it. Finding two or three different anti-psoriasis medications and interchanging them frequently will help keep the skin disease off balance.

Fishing for Hope

Recent studies of a fish oil called maxEPA on psoriasis patients have shown that 60 percent of them experienced marked improvement in their scaling, redness and itching. Check out your health food store for fish oil supplements and try them for a couple of months. Also, adding more fish to your diet will give you a more pure, direct source of the kind of fish oil you need.

Reduce your stress

Psoriasis almost always responds directly to stress — that is, the more stress you have in your life the worse it gets. Psoriasis flare-ups accompany times of pressure and emotional upheaval in your life. Reducing the amount of stress you have on a daily basis may provide a lot of relief. Of course, this could mean anything from changing jobs to divorcing your spouse! It all depends on you and your individual life situation. Perhaps it time to make a decision about how you want to be living your life.

Soothing Sunbaths

Perhaps one of the best things about having psoriasis — if there ever could be anything good about it — is that it gives you an excellent excuse to bask in some sunshine or a tanning salon booth. Ultra-violet radiation has long been recognized as a way to decrease the severity of psoriasis. Even if your psoriasis occurs only beneath your hair, or in some other relatively unexposed area of your body, the light of a tanning booth or the sun will have a positive effect on the problem no matter where it occurs. Combine that with the fact that psoriatic people may have increased immunity to skin cancer, and you have all the reason in the world to walk around looking tanned and rested.

A Zen approach to psoriasis:
Acceptance without resignation

Zen monks have long taught their students that to have an attitude toward life which states that one should accept the world as it is, but not resign to it. There is a big difference between accepting a certain reality that you don't like, and just giving into it.

For example, tearing out your hair and being miserable over the fact that we have poverty, famine and starvation in the world rarely does any good because these things have always been a part of the human experience and probably always will be. To deny the reality of it all does little good. Instead, one should accept the fact that not everything about life is good, but at the same time, maintain the attitude that you can do something about it.

As Jesus said: "The poor will always be with us." But that doesn't mean you shouldn't help them out — right?

The same attitude should be taken toward your psoriasis. You should accept the fact that you may never get rid of it entirely. Doing so will reduce your level of stress and disappointment about your disease. It will also prevent you from getting frustrated or depressed about your psoriasis. Once you have accepted the reality of it, you can expend more energy trying to deal with it.

Olive Oil

Olive oil can be effective is helping psoriasis from becoming too dry and flakey. Especially when your scalp is the main area of infection, dabbing your head with olive oil at night will help your skin retain moisture. A shampoo the next morning with a good coal tar shampoo to wash out the oil will leave your scalp refreshed and in much better shape than it was the night before. Olive oil before bedtime is especially effective during dry winter seasons when psoriasis can get so much worse. Sesame oil is another great oil, and it has less odor than olive oil.

P&S Liquid

One of the most effective — perhaps the most effective — products to remove psoriatic scales is something called P&S Liquid, which you can buy without a prescription. Apply it at night and wash it off in the morning. The only drawback is that it is very messy and can irriate the skin, so don't use it more than once or twice a week.

Dermatologists have a lot of stuff

If you have psoriasis you'll probably end up in a doctor's office sooner or later out of shear frustration as you seek new ways to fight your skin problem. Dermatologists have an incredible battery of drugs, creams and lotions for psoriasis. Many of them work better than over-the-counter products, but the big problem with them is that you need to keep going back to the doctor for your prescription. This can become quite a problem, especially with psoriasis, because the trouble of making an appointment, visting a doctor and getting a prescrition filled (an often expensive prescription) can wear you down. Because yo have to take care of psoriasis every day, every added ritual seems to become more and more diffcult to perform. So, the moral of this little story is, visit your doctor — he or she can really help — but keeping up with your psoriasis via a doctor can be just as frustrating as anything else.

Some other skin rashes and problems of note

Skin rashes can jump out at you from some very unlikely sources. Here are a few to be aware of:

Frostbite — Skin that is exposed to extreme cold, especially combined with wind, can suffer significant, sometimes permanent damage unless the right precautions are taken.

Exposed areas, such as cheeks and nose, or extremities, such as fingers and toes, are most prone to frostbite. You may not feel it at first, but when you come in out of the cold you'll notice a burning sensation in the affected areas. Superficial frostbite is characterized by pale, whitish spots on the skin, or numbness in the fingers and toes.

Common sense tells you that frostbitten skin should be warmed up as soon as possible, and common sense is correct. As long as the affected area is exposed to cold the area of damage will get bigger and worse. If you can, go indoors right away and apply warm water or a warm, wet compress where you need it. The sooner you catch it, the better off you'll be. Do not rub the frostbitten area. Friction is the last thing you need because the skin is already tender and damaged. Rubbing your hands together will make frostbite worse.

As frostbite gets deeper, it causes more permanent damage, and can even result in loss of fingers, toes, arms or legs. The only remedy is to get warm or find shelter as soon as possible. If you have severe frostbite, you need to see a doctor because gangrene will set in quickly and result in the loss of a limb or death.

Various soaps and bubble baths — Chemcials used in many soaps can cause rashes, or even dermatitis. Soaking in a long bubble bath can ber a very likely sourse of skin reactions.

Nickles — That's right, the metal. It seems that nickel — in watches, buttons, jewelry and in other items that make contact with your skin — can cause a kind of dermatitis. If you have an itch or rash next to a nickel item, get rid of it.

Going nuts? — A great many people have allergies to nuts. Nut allergies seem to often manifest themselves in skin rashes. Keep an eye on your skin activity after you eat nuts, especially cashews. Cashews, in fact, are akin to the poison ivy plant. If you eat cashew nuts that have not been thoroughly cleaned, especially their outer shells, you may be getting the same skin irritant you would find in poison ivy, poison oak or poison sumac.

Stress

It's as simple as this: Stress in the inability to cope with your every day life — or the price you pay for getting by when you do cope.

Most often you do get by. You cope. And the person who has not been stressed has not lived. But that doesn't mean being stressed all the time is a good thing.

But, really, you don't need a book to tell you what stress is , you are probably all-too-familiar with it. So many things can cause stress these days — money problems, family problems, your job, your children, your health, your relationship, fear of crime, and on and on.

But how does stress affect our health? Does it cause some sort of chemical change in our bodies that can make us sick? The answer is yes. Here is how it works:

External events in your life and environment cause your body to react in certain ways. The way you react to stress develops over a long period of time, and also is determined by evolution and the way our bodies have learned to adapt to the environment over thousands of years.

One of the most common stress producing external events is a source of danger or fear. If you are attacked by a mugger or a vicious dog, for example, your body will produce adrenaline and other hormones to help you "fight or flee." But, as it turns out, it doesn't have to be something as dramatic as an attack or life-threatening event to produce the "fight or flight" mechanism in your body. Being called on the carpet by your boss, being fired, getting divorced and similar events also put your body into maximum defense mode. If you have a high stress job, for example, with a lot of deadlines and pressure to perform well, you may be doing the physiological equivalent of fleeing a saber-toothed tiger every day.

The problem is, your body was not designed to fight for it's life once a day. The result is the harmful effects of stress. Adrenaline in your body can result in the release of corticosteroids and the depletion of norepinephrine in your body. This can cause depression and degrade the performance of your immune system — which in turn leaves your body open to attack from any number of viruses, bacteria, environmental toxins and systemic conditions.

Fortunately, there are many things you can do to counteract the chemical changes in your body by eating the proper food and taking the right vitamin and food supplements. The following may help you a lot.

Combine Vitamins B-6 and C With Phenylalanine to
Fight Stress and Depression

Vitamins B-6 and C are two of the major stress fighters because they help convert certain amino acids, including a protein called phenylalanine in your body into norepinephrine, which helps balance and boost your immune system. Taking adequate amounts of these vitamins will also fight depression.

Foods that are rich in phenylalanine include:

apples	pineapples
beets	carrots
parsley	spinach
tomatoes	soymilk
tofu	nutritional yeast

Vitamins A and Zinc Boost the Immune System

To help fight off the stress on an injury, it is important to bolster the thymus gland, which some call the "master gland" of the immune system. The thymus gland shrinks as people, especially men, get older and Vitamin A and Zinc prevent the shrinking process.

Bolster Your Sense of Self Respect

Having a low opinion of yourself is one of the main reasons people find themselves unable to cope with their lives. Obviously, if you have no faith or confidence in yourself, even the simplest events are producers of stress because you perceive yourself as constantly in losing situations.

One of the best ways to bolster self esteem is to realize that you probably accomplish much more than you think you do, even if only in small ways. Take a minute to list all the positive accomplishments you perform in a single day. Even if it's just getting the laundry done or washing the dishes, that is an extremely important accomplishment. You know what your house looks like when you let things like that go. So if you just get up right now and get the dishes done — you're on your way to higher self esteem and a lower stress level. Always give your focus to what you have done, not what you have failed to do.

If you need to, join a self help group. Go for one hour per week so you can just let go and talk and listen to the problems of other people. One of the best ways to bolster your own self esteem is to listen to the problems of others. It's an absolute guarantee that you'll find many other people with problems a lot worse than your own — and since those people are coping — you'll realize that you can too.

Have a Regular Diversion

If your stress comes from a 50, 60 or 70-hour work week, you should find some regular form of escape. At the very least, you should have one day off per week where you have no responsibilities whatsoever, not even family or personal responsibilities. If you spend 90 percent of your energy on work, and the remaining 10 percent taking care of your family or social life, you'll soon be 100 percent dead — and then nothing will be taken care of. Take Sundays off to do nothing! It's as simple as that! It may spare you a heart attack.

Naps are Great

No one in the world is so busy that he or she can't sneak a 15-minute nap somewhere into the day, sometimes twice a day. Even the President of the United States finds time for a quick nap. If a man with the weight of an entire country's problems on his shoulders can find time for a nap, certainly you can too.

Exercise

Unless you've been living in cave for the past 100 years you already know that a regular, daily session of exercise, such as a walk, a run, a quick game of basketball at noon, a swim, a bike ride, or any other exercise has been shown to not only help emotionally, but also dramatically reduce the harmful chemical changes the body undergoes during times of stress. It's time for you to really try this old advice to an old problem. What's holding you back?

Some Other 100 Percent Guaranteed Stress Reducers

These need no explanation, but they all have been shown to counteract and kill stress dead in its tracks. See how many of them you can pick up or do more of in your life:

fall in love	compromise more
laugh	slow down
meditate	be kind to an animal
avoid loneliness	avoid self pity
practice deep breathing	Shout as loud as you can (when alone)

(Note: see sections under accupressure and meditation for some excellent anti-stress techniques).

Strokes

A stroke is a rupture of a blood vessel, or formation of a clot that interferes with circulation. A stroke is not a heart attack, and should not be confused with a heart problem. Strokes happen in your brain.

A stroke in the brain, commonly called a CVA (cerebrovascular accident) can be tiny, minor and hardly noticeable, or it can devastate a person completely, causing paralysis, blindness, loss of speech and ability to swallow, dimentia, coma or death.

Something very similar to stroke is called TIA, or transient ischemic attack. This occurs when too little blood flow reaches the brain without a complete stroke occurring. The symptoms of TIA are seeing double for a few minutes, or temporary loss of vision in one eye. TIA may also produce temporary weakness or paralysis of a limb or loss of speech — all of which clear up as suddenly as they come on.

Let's talk more about strokes and how to handle them. First, TIA.

Transient Ischemic Attack

If you experience TIA, it is a clear warning sign that you are in danger of something worse, possibly a stroke. If you experience a TIA as described above, the first thing you should do it take two aspirins to thin your blood and help stop further clotting. You probably should also take an aspirin a day for the rest of your life to ward off further problems.

Remember that TIA is a warning that the real thing could happen. That real thing is stroke. If you experience TIA, get yourself to a doctor as soon as possible.

Stroke

Both TIA and strokes are the result of weaknesses and problems with the arteries in your body, in this case, with the arteries that serve your brain. The biggest culprit is arteriosclerosis, which is hardening of the arteries and the gradual narrowing of the openings in the arteries. When an artery blocks completely, the result is a build up of blood that is trying to get through and an eventual break of the artery. When that happens, brain tissue is also damaged, which causes the paralysis, mental disturbances and other problems.

Another way strokes happen is by the relentless pounding of high blood pressure against an artery. Many people have high blood pressure without knowing it, so a stroke can happen when you least expect it. Also, if you develop a blood clot in some other part of your body, the leg, for example, that clot can eventually find its way to the brain and cause a stroke.

Prevention is the key

Strokes are bad news and the best way to deal with them is to never have one. There is much you can start doing today to ensure your veins and arteries stay healthy enough, and that your blood pressure stays low enough, so that you never experience the devastation of a stroke.

First of all, avoid the big four — cholesterol, tobacco, alcohol and salt. The more high fat food you eat, the more your arteries clog and harden and the more prone you will be to stroke. See the "cholesterol" heading in this book for a number of tips and methods that will help you get your cholesterol level under control. The same goes for blood pressure. One of the number one contributors to high blood pressure is too much fat and alcohol in your diet, as well as salt, sodium and all other forms of sodium products. Have your blood pressure checked on a regular basis. If you are too high, take steps to bring it down or you're heading for a stroke sooner or later. Of course, smoking is a primary cause of arterial disease. Tobacco wreaks havoc on your blood vessels, making them weaker and poisoning your blood. It also robs your brain of oxygen which it sorely needs to fight off strokes. So, in general, clean up your act, and you'll immediately take yourself out of running for a gold medal at the stroke-a-thon of life event.

If a stroke happens

How do you tell if someone has suffered a stroke? Symptoms are paralysis or sudden weakness on one side of the body, inability to speak, difficulty in breathing or swallowing and unconsciousness. Just before a stroke hits, the person may become confused, agitated or disoriented.

A small stroke can cause headache, dizziness, confusion, and a few days later, difficulty in speech, weakness in an arm or leg on one side and memory or personality changes.

If you suspect a person has suffered a stroke you should:

(1) Don't fool around. Get them to a doctor immediately. The person's life may be on the line, and permanent damage will become worse the longer the victim goes untreated.

(2) Maintain an open airway in the person and place the person on his or her side to that secretions can drain from the mouth.

(3) Give rescue breathing if necessary.

(4) Keep the victim at rest.

If the stroke is a minor one you should:

(1) Protect the person against accident or physical exertion. A person who has suffered a minor stroke may want to act in bizarre ways or say strange things. Just make sure they don't do anything to harm themselves.

(2) Try to keep the patient at rest, although this may be

difficult if the person is agitated. Keep the person as still as possible without resorting to a physical struggle to hold him or her down.

After a stroke

As bad as strokes are, many people can recover from them fully, while others may have symptoms of paralysis, loss of speech or vision and other problems for the rest of their lives.

One must make strenuous efforts to avoid the things that caused the stroke in the first place. If a person continues to smoke after a stroke, and many people do, the chances of having another, more serious CVA increase by many times. Also, stroke victims need to take aspirin or other blood thinners every day for the rest of their lives.

Many stroke victims require the help of a speech therapist and physical therapists to bring back body functions that were lost to paralysis. But the point is, your body can come back from a serious stroke, and you can prevent yourself from having further strokes. It's all up to you. Throw out those cigarettes, cut back on the booze and salt, and learn to appreciate a more quiet mode of life.

Throat problems

About 80 percent of all sore throats are caused by viral infections or irritants from smoking, shouting, coughing and postnasal drainage — unless it is a bacterial infection, in which case you have strep throat, and then you have a real humdinger of a sore throat.

A diagnosis of strep throat can only be made — for sure —

by taking a sample of mucus from the throat and growing it in a petri dish for 48 hours. Then a hospital lab technologist will use his microscope to identify strep bacteria. If the test is positive, then you have strep throat.

But here are three signs that may indicate you actually have strep throat:

(a) Yellow or white mucus that may give a "cobblestone" appearance to the throat.

(b) Swollen lymph nodes along the jaw and in the front of the throat.

(c) Fever.

If you think you have strep throat, you should remember that you can easily infect others, so be careful about personal contact, sharing drinking glasses, towels, etc.

Usually, you need an antibiotic prescribed by a doctor to fight off bacterial strep infections.

Other sore throats

If your sore throat is not a strep infection, there is much you can do on your own to fight it off and make yourself feel better. Here's a list of things you can do:

(1) Gargle every two hours to relieve pain and clear away mucous. The best solution is one teaspoon of salt with 8 oz of warm water.

(2) Take frequent sips of hot liquid. Lemon tea is excellent, as are fruits juices, especially citrus juices, such as orange and grapefruit juice.

(3) Monitor temperature closely for signs of fever.

(4) Swallow some aspirins, but don't gargle with them. That can cause further irritation of your throat.

(5) Use zinc lozenges — they have been linked to stopping many cold-like viral infections dead in their tracks.

(6) Bed rest will conserve your healing energies.

(7) Stop smoking.

(8) Don't use your voice any more than you have to. Definitely no shouting. You'll be sorry if you do.

Moisturize the room

Keeping the air in the room moist will keep your throat from getting dry and scratchy. Always keep a humidifier running, especially in the winter, or put a bowl of water on the radiator. Be sure to always keep your humidifier squeeky clean because it can easily be a breeding ground for molds, fungus and bacteria that can further attack your throat.

Laryngitis

Speaking of a dry throat, laryngitis, or loss of voice, is a common problem associated with colds, sore throats and dry throats.

One of the best ways to get your voice back is frequent moisturization of your vocal cords with water and juices. It will help get your cords back into shape.

Shut up!

Sometimes your body tries to tell you things — and if you lose your voice, you body is pretty much hoping that you'll shut your gab for a while. By refraining from use of your voice, you'll allow your throat and vocal cords to heal quickly. If you don't, you may cause a long-term problem that will rob you of your voice for weeks.

Also, just keeping your mouth closed will prevent air from getting at your pipes and drying them out further. Breathe through your nose, keep quiet and just give your vocal cords a couple of days to heal. Your golden voice will be gracing the airways again before you know it.

Touch Power!

Does the simple power of human touch in the form of massage have the power to heal? We all know a massage feels good, but is there a benefit beyond that?

According to University of Miami researchers, the answer is — yes!

Researchers at the university investigated the effects of massage on AIDS, cancer, addiction,and the relationship between touch and physical and emotional development. So far, the findings have been far beyond what was expected.

For example, premature "crack babies" who were given 15-minute massages three times a day for 10 days had fewer postnatal complicaitons, a 28 percent daily weight gain, and markedly more mature motor behaviors at the end of the 10-day period.

AIDS patients who received a 45-minute massage five times weekly for a month exhibited improved immune function and a significant reduction in anxiety and distress levels.

Abused children living in shelters became more active and sociable when they were massaged. Massaged preschoolers become less fidgety and more concentrated. Officer workers that were massaged became less tired and more alert.

Massage, it seems, increases the level of serotonin in the brain. Serotonin is a neurotransmitter which facilitates the release of natural body defense cells.

Researchers point out that these finding are only preliminary, but clearly demonstrate the exciting potential of something as simple and affordable as a massage. Furthermore, the full potential of massage has yet to be explored. For the sake of your own health, or for those whom you love, how about trying out a regular, daily massage on each other? At the very least, it'll feel great; at best, it will bolster your immune system, help you fight off disease, or make your current good health even better!

Ulcers

Most of us casually assume these days that ulcers are caused by stress and anxiety, and that if we could just take it easy and stop worrying so much, things would get better.

Maybe.

Today, the cause of a stomach or colon ulcer is still a source of controversy. The bottom line is that too much acid in the stomach is what causes a sore to open up in the stomach lining, which may bleed, cause tremendous pain and heartburn, and generally make your life miserable. Ulcers can also cause indigestion, nausea, vomiting, black stool and other problems. Certain foods really cause ulcers to act up, and which foods those are depends on the person.

Too much coffee, booze and using too many aspirins probably have more to do with ulcers than does a high-stress lifestyle. Common sense tells you that if you have an ulcer, you should avoid coffee, alcohol, sweets and tobacco, and common sense is entirely correct.

A bland food diet?

Traditionally, doctors have put people with ulcers on bland-food diets of milk, no spices, low fats and grease, and an assorted other bunch of mush.

Well, the good news is that bland food diets are no longer seen as being effective in battling an ulcer. In fact, milk is one of the worst things you can put into your stomach if you have an ulcer! Studies show that milk actually increases the amount of acid in your stomach, rather than coating and soothing. Another study showed that people with ulcers who drank milk every day became worse as a result. So if you have an ulcer, avoid milk.

Rather than going on a bland diet, it's a better idea to find out which foods irritate you specifically, and avoid them. Certain food which you may be purposefully avoiding may actually be good for an ulcer. Such foods as garlic and onions, for example, may be good for your ulcer despite their powerful reputations. Do a little experimenting. Keep a food log. You'll soon discover what sets you off and what is safe.

What else to avoid

The pause that refreshes — Besides coffee, booze and sugar, you should make a strong effort to avoid soft drinks, especially Coke and Pepsi. Both contain high amounts of sugar and moderate amounts of caffeine — two of the worst possible things for your stomach. Studies have shown that Coke drastically increases the amount of acid in the stomach and duodenum, the two areas most prone to ulceration. Coke not only makes an ulcer much worse, but may be one of the main causes of ulcers in America. The same is true for most other soft drinks.

Pain killers — Another stomach bomb is the common aspirin, and other aspirin-like drugs, such as NSAIDs. NSAIDs are anti-inflammatory medicines used for a variety of purposes, including arthritis and other inflammatory diseases. If you are prone to a lot of headaches which you treat with aspirins, or if you take prescription NSAIDs, you may be flirting with an ulcer, so watch it. Get the advice of a doctor on this.

Salt— Although still controversial, salt is being increasingly linked to ulcers and to making them worse. Reduce the salt in your diet and see what happens.

Tobacco — It's the worst! It not only doubles your chance of getting an ulcer, but if you already have one, it will wreak untold pain and suffering upon you, and may turn your ulcer into stomach cancer. If you have an ulcer and you smoke, you are truly a time-bomb waiting to explode. Do whatever you can to kick the habit, or your stomach will kick you out of the game of life.

What will help

Antacids — Your doctor has lots of drugs for ulcers, but you can do a lot on your own to ease the pain and help your stomach or colon heal. Over-the-counter antacids are simply a good remedy. They reduce the amount of acid in your stomach, and that's what ulcers are all about — too much acid in your stomach.

Eat Right — Eating stomach-friendly foods that are easy to digest will treat your stomach with kid gloves while it makes its comeback. A vegetarian diet by far is better than a diet with a lot of meats and dairy products. But you don't have to go totally vegetarian. Just make sure you get a lot of fiber and other foods that aid digestion, such as brown rice, potatoes, bran, broccoli, beans, apples and so on.

De-stress yourself — I know, we already said that stress and anxiety probably don't cause ulcers as it has long been thought, but stress definitely increases the trauma of an ulcer. Mental stress on the job or in your personal life causes more acid to form in your stomach, just the opposite of what you want to ease the open wound of an ulcer. An excellent way to de-stress is with a daily 10-minute session of meditation and with exercise.

Instead of taking a greasy lunch break at McDonalds, perhaps you should pack a brown bag lunch of some easy-to-eat and digest fruits and vegetables, and eat them while you take a walk or visit a museum. How you de-stress yourself is up to you. You'll have to find a way to fit more rest, relaxation and meditation into your lifestyle. But the double whammy of an easy-to-digest diet with reduced stress in your daily life can heal up an ulcer for good with nary a visit to the doctor's office.

Vaccination Alert!

Is getting your child vaccinated for common diseases like measles and mumps a good idea?

Of course! you might answer automatically — but don't be so sure.

Modern medicine considers the development of vaccines for diseases as polio, diphtheria, measles, mumps, rubella, tetanus and whooping cough — as a virtual triumph over biological enemies that have killed or crippled billions of people throughout history.

Most of us routinely — and without question — have our children vaccinated against whatever microscopic dangers our public health specialists warn us about.

But is there a dark side to vaccination?

Yes, say an increasing number of medical professionals who think that an overload of vaccinations are compromising the natural immune system of the human population, and may be harming the health of individual people.

Consider this:

Doctors inoculate some 60,000 children per week; nearly 100 percent of these children have had seven to nine different vaccinations — which include an injected mixture of 27 different disease antigens — all by the age of 18 months. Most get all of their shots between the ages of two months and two years.

Some of those vaccinations result in the death of children, may cause brain damage, learning disabilities, mental retardation and impaired immune systems.

One vaccination in particular — DPT, which is administered for pertussis, diptheria and tetanus — has been singles out for a number of deadly side effects. According to a study for every 3.3 million infants who receive the DPT vaccination each year, 4,248 have post-injection convulsive or collapse; 10,377 have high-pitched screaming within 48 hours and 18,873 infants have some form of significant neurological reaction within two days. About one in 875 DPT shots result in shock, convulsion or collapse.

The adverse effects and symptoms can be as diverse as the multitude of injected anti-disease agents.

But aren't getting vaccines worth the risk? Aren't the risks to a small percentage of the population better than getting the diseases themsleves?

Not necessarily. Vaccines, as it turns out, may be making our children and general population more susceptible to even worse disease later on in life such as AIDS and other immuno-deficieny diseases.

Common childhood diseases such as mumps, chicken pox and measles can actually be beneficial experiences in a child's immunological health and shouldn't be prevented. While a child's body fights off these diseases, the body is developing and array of natural defenses — defenses which a child may not have later on in life if they never develop them.

Instead of preventing such diseases with vaccines, some doctors argue that natural, homepathic and herbal remedies should be applied that will lessen the severity of the disease, while at the same time, allowing immunological systems in the child to form.

To find out which homeopathic or herbal remedies are appropriate for particular conditions, you should seek the help of a homeopathic medicine specialist. Your local health food store owner will be able to steer you in the right direction.

The bottom line is, vaccinations are something you should take a second look at. Perhaps not all of the vaccinations your doctor recommends are necessary. Or, if your child has suddenly developed a mysterious disease of some kind, perhaps the kind of vaccination recently administered will provide a clue to the problem and help your doctor find treatment.

Be warned: this is an extremely controversial topic. Many schools do not allow the admittance of children who are not immunized. In most states it is illegal to refuse vaccinations, although all 50 states allow an exemption based on medical contradications. That requires a note from a licensed medical doctor. An exemption based on religious beliefs is allowed in 48 states, In 22 states a philisophical exemption is allowed, and can be obtained by a simple note from a parent.

Before you make a decision on vaccinations one way or another, do your homework. Doa lot of thinking. Don't do anything that would endanger your child. Consult as many experts on the subject as you can. Ultimately, your health and that of your child is in your own hands. It's up to you to decide what's best.

Vaginitis
(including yeast infections)

Vaginitis is an inflammation of the mucous surface of the vagina, the vagina lips and the glands and tissues surrounding it. The most common cause is infection by fungus, parasites and bacteria, such as strep, staph, coliform and others. Perhaps the most common form of vaginal infection is the dreaded yeast infection.

Whatever the source of attack, the result is a discharge, itching, burning and even pain and unpleasant odor.

Avoid the causes

Vaginal infections result from a lowered resistance due to sickness, lack of rest and sleep, frequent stress, a poor diet and insufficient intake of liquids. Other causes are oral contraceptives which alter the acidity of the vaginal area, nylon underwear or other materials which retain moisture and promote growth of fungus.

Discharge can be cottage cheese like, thin and foamy, yellowish green or gray in color.

Eat some yogurt

Yogurt is especially popular with women, for good reason. It will replace certain helpful bacteria in your stomach that will be killed by prescriptions for killing yeast infections, which you get from your doctor or over the counter. Any antibiotic may cause a woman to have more yeast infections because the drug will kill as many good bacteria as bad.

Don't douche with yogurt! Douching with yogurt to kill yeast injections is a popular, apocryphal method in many circles. But douching with yogurt will not cure a yeast infection and may give you some other sexually transmitted disease.

Avoid sugars and dairy products

Eating a lot of sweets is the very thing that yeast cells love. Yeast cells are a very common cause of vaginal infection. Eating garlic, on the other hand, is known to kill yeast cells in your system. So avoid the sweets, starches and dairy products, but increase your intake of garlic.

Vinegar douches

Use 1 oz. of vinegar in one quart of warm water. Apply the douche while lying on your back in the bathtub and suspend the douche well above your body. Insert the tube well into the vagina and release the clamp, allowing the solution to flow freely within. Clamp the tube and sit up to allow the vagina to drain. Repeat the process until one or two quarts of the solution have been used up.

Other treatment tips:

(1) Avoid scratching because it will makes things worse and will make your infection spread.

(2) Don't wear clothes that are tight in the crotch and thighs.

(3) If you have a doctor's prescription, make sure you take all of it, even after symptoms disappear.

(4) Abstain from sexual intercourse until your medicine is gone and you are free of symptoms.

Prevention

Some women are just prone to yeast infection and other vaginal problems. Here are some tips to avoid recurrent problems with yeast infection.

Super clean underwear

Remember that yeast and other bacteria are extremely tiny and can cling to life in even the most microscopic nooks and crannies that make up the fiber of your undergarments. Just as the only sure way to kill harmful bacteria in water is to boil it, the same treatment may be necessary for your underwear. That's right — boil your underwear. It may not do much for their shelf-life, but it sure as heck will kill every single varmint that's hiding within.

Wear loose-fitting clothing to give your vaginal area a chance to breath and stay dry. You don't want to give yeast the dark, dank conditions they need to multiply.

Avoid chemicals and foreign substances of all sorts

From spermicides to perfumes and douches, any chemical or deodorant you apply to yourself can lead to some sort of problem. If you are prone to vaginal infection, don't flirt with disaster. Keep it clean and simple. Don't use talcum powder either. It can not only cause problems, but also lead to cancer of the vagina, according to some studies.

Varicose Veins

Varicose veins are a cousin to another problem with swollen, distended veins — hemorrhoids. Both are caused by pressures on veins which cause them to bulge out into the skin where they take on a bluish or purple look, cause pain, and can lead to other problems, such as blood clots and serious pain. Varicose veins sometimes require surgical removal, but most often can be dealt with less drastically.

Battling varicose veins is all about pressure and gravity. Common sense tells you that the veins in your legs can be pumped up with a lot of pressure in a variety of situations. The pressure of pregnancy and giving birth is an obvious source of the kind of pressures that push out veins. But other more insidious forces can be at work as well. If you sit at a desk all day, or cross your legs a lot, you can be bulging out the veins in your legs, weakening them and promoting varicose veins.

Getting rid of varicose veins involves doing the opposite of what brings them on — that is, reducing the amount of gravity and pressure on your legs.

Equal and opposite reaction

Isaac Newton told us that for every action, there is an equal and opposite reaction. Applying pressure against the outward thrust of varicose veins will help them shrink back down. Buy elastic support stockings that will hug your legs and force blood back out of the veins. You can buy support stockings in any department store and you can get different levels of support. You don't need to buy the tightest. Moderate elasticity will help you out while causing you the least discomfort.

By the same token, tight fitting clothes above your body will force more blood downward into your legs, which you don't want to happen. Don't wear girdles that squeeze your waste or torso, or tight fitting jeans and underwear.

Reducing gravity

Propping up your legs above the rest of your body for several minutes several times a day will give your veins a chance to rest and go back down to normal size. Propping up your legs allows the blood to flow away from your legs and out into your torso and head. Also, you may want to put some blocks under your bed to make sure your legs are raised slightly all night, keeping pressure off of them.

Lose some weight

This is one of those real common sense things that you

know will work if you try it. Losing weight takes a lot or pressure and weight off your legs — it's as simple as that. Also, less weight means you'll have lower blood pressure, which can only help varicose veins.

Keep yourself moving as much as possible

Just as sitting for long periods of time is a major cause of hemorrhoids, the same is true with varicose veins. Sitting at your desk all day with your legs crossed, or with your feet propped up on the legs of your chair with your knees bent tight is just asking for bulging veins in your legs. Get up at least every two hours, stretch and walk around for 15 minutes to take the pressure off and get the blood flow going.

Remember ...

Varicose veins can be more than a cosmetic problem. If serious clotting occurs in a varicose vein, you should seek the attention of a doctor to have the vein dealt with surgically. Sometimes just a few minutes of out-patient surgery can have you back on your feet within just an hour or two and you will have relief from the pain and cramping in your legs.

Yeast Infection

When you hear yeast infection, you probably think: "female problem." And it is true that vaginal yeast infections are a very common problem, and that women have been dealing with this nuisance for centuries.

But yeast may be a far bigger culprit for both men and women than previously thought.

Do you have a lot of skin rashes? Are you bothered frequently by constipation, bloating, asthma and headaches? Are you more fatigued than you should be? Are you depressed and nervous for no good reason?

There's a good possibility it may all be due to yeast, not vaginal yeast, but intestinal yeast.

A particular yeast cell, known as candida, exists naturally in the human intestine, along with dozens of other bacteria, most of which are benficial. In fact, the microscopic denizens of your intestines comprise a delicate balance which, if not properly maintained, can result in the problems mentioned above.

Yeast cells can grow out of control in your intestines if its competing bacteria are killed off by anti-biotics, an improper diet, or any one of a half-dozen other medications or conditions.

When yeast cells multiply out of control, they begin secreting large amounts of harmful toxins throughout your body by seeping into your bloodstream, reaking havoc everywhere.

How to get rid of intentinal yeast

Two things you can do right away to reduce the candida population in your intestinal tract is to take daily doses of garlic, and stop eating sweets.

Garlic has long been known for its benefical and medicinal properties, and it is an especially good cleanser of stomach and intestines. Experienced travelers, for example, have long known that the negative affects of local water supplies — including diarrhea and dysentery — can be prevented with frequent, large doses of garlic. Garlic, as it turns out, is an excellent antifungal agent, espescially garlic cloves or garlic powder.

Yeast cells love sugar, so the more you eat the more the yeast inside you will thrive. This includes not only candy, but the many things we eat everyday that contain sugar — everything from bread to salad dressing.

In addition to sweets, you should also avoid moldy fruits; fungi products, such as mushrooms; cheese; and fermented foods, such as alcohol, vinegar and soy sauce.

On the other hand, you should eat plenty of freshly prepared, well cooked foods, with an emphasis on fruits, vegetables and rice. Avoid raw foods that are hard to digest, such as broccoli and cauliflower. Don't eat anything after 7 p.m.

Foods that reduce intestinal yeast

Garlic	pearl barley
corn	dried ginger
pumpkin	scallions
rice	ginseng tea

Why massage is important to treat yeast infection

Massaging your bodies with certain oils — especially linsead oil — will stimulate and open the pores in your skin, and improve their ability to pass the toxins out of your body. Once you start taking garlic and reduce your sugar intake, yeast cells will begin dying off rapidly,and they will need to be excreted from your body. A good, regular massage will help that process.

Mental Exercise that battle yeast infection

You can reprogram your mind and your subconscious mind to be more resistent to fungal infestions in your body, such as yeast.

Once a day, look at your self in the mirror and come up with some positive statements about yourself and life in general, and repeat them a number of times. Try this: "My body is cleansing itself, and can easily resist any unwanted toxin or invader." Or: Every cell of my body is radiating light — I glow with good health." Or: I love myself and others and I deserve a happy, healthy life."

So you can fight your yeast infection on three fronts:

(1) Blast yeast cells with a large, daily intake of garlic — it will kill yeast cells by the million! Eat foods that absorb moisture and inrcease immunity.

(2) Avoid the foods that help yeast cells along — sweets, moldy foods, any raw or uncooked foods.

(3) Strengthen your mental and emotional resolve to fight off internal toxins and disease. Give yourself positive affirmation in the mirror everyday.

Water

Is your tap water tainted? Maybe you should find out. It's no longer a given in America that the turn of a faucet will produce clean, chemically safe, uncontaminated drinking water. Everything from farm chemicals to forgotten, underground leaky gas tanks have bled into the water supply of many an unsuspecting population.

There are many ways to get your water tested. All you have to do is look in the yellow pages for a company that will perform such a test for you. Or you can call a local university, or any firm which deals in chemical processing for a referral as to where you can get your water tested. Such a test is usually less than $20.

There's no need to panic. The vast majority of water in America is safe to drink — but even water that is currently considered safe is now being re-examined for its long-term safety. In some studies, chlorine - a universal additive in public water supplies to sterilize water — has been linked with higher levels of cancer. Beyond that, many food and nutrition experts consider ALL tap water to be too laden with unnatural chemicals to be safe over the long run.

It would be difficult to underestimate the importance of fresh, pure water on your overall health. After all, your body is 80 to 90 percent water! That's what you are — a lot of water with a few additives to hold it together and make you feel solid. In fact, brain cells are particularly high in water content, and optimum moisture and purity levels in your brain can make a huge difference in your life.

Despite its importance, most people do not drink enough water. Taking notice of your water intake and keeping your body adequately supplied can be a key factor in your health. Those that routinely deprive themselves of adequate water may find a higher level of health return to them magically — just by drinking more water!

And we're not talking about any water here. To ensure you are putting the very best water in your body, we recommend water that has been distilled via the process of reverse osmosis. Where do you find that kind of water? Easy! Go to your supermarket and check out the labels on the various bottled water products. All of them list clearly on their lables whether or not they were distilled via revrese osmosis.

If you want to spend more money in the short term, but save money in the long term, you can buy your own reverse osmosis distilling machine. They cost $300 to $500 but can easily supply you with 10 gallons of purified drinking water per day. At that rate, your distilling device would pay for itself in less than a year.

Just remember to drink when you are thirsty — don't ignore it or let it go. And don't always try satisfying your thirst with something other than water. As you know, coffee and soft drinks will make you deplete your water levels as fast as you can replenish them. Even healthy drinks, such as fruit and vegetable juices, are not a perfect substitute for water. Somtimes the simplest things separate us from a life of good health and a life of pain and suffering. A daily dose of fresh water may be the only thing you need to turn your health around!

NOTES

INDEX

OTHER HEALTH AND MONEY BOOKS

The following books are offered to our preferred customers at a special price.

BOOK   ## PRICE

1. Health Secrets $26.95 POSTPAID
2. Money Tips $26.95 POSTPAID
3. The Guidebook of Insiders Tips $9.95   POSTPAID
4. Proven Health Tips Encyclopedia $11.97 POSTPAID
5. Foods That Heal $19.95 POSTPAID
6. Healing & Prevention Secrets $26.95 POSTPAID
7. Most Valuable Book Ever Published $9.95   POSTPAID
8. The Smart Money Guide $9.95   POSTPAID

Please send this entire page or write down the names of the books and mail it along with your payment

NAME OF BOOK_____PRICE_____
NAME OF BOOK_____PRICE_____
NAME OF BOOK_____PRICE_____
NAME OF BOOK_____PRICE_____

TOTAL ENCLOSED$_____

SHIP TO:
Name_____
Address_____
City_____ST_____Zip_____

MAIL TO: AMERICAN PUBLISHING CORPORATION
BOOK DISTRIBUTION CENTER
POST OFFICE BOX 15196
MONTCLAIR, CA 91763-5196